MARY MAGDALENE'S DAUGHTER

The Story of Sarah

PIA ORLEANE, PH.D.

PUBLISHED BY ONEWATER PRESS

Mary Magdalene's Daughter ~ The Story of Sarah
by Pia Orleane, Ph.D.

Copyright © 2023 Pia Orleane, Ph.D and
Cullen Baird Smith
Published by Onewater Press

Book and cover design by BookSavvyStudio.com

ISBN: 978-1-7367035-3-3 (paperback)
ISBN: 978-1-7367035-2-6 (eBook)

Printed in the United States of America

*I dedicate this book to my true divine family:
Sarah, who gave me this story, Mother Mary,
Mary Magdalene, and Jesus of Nazareth, and to the divine
that lives in each of us and guides us when we listen fully
to our hearts. We are all divine beings. Choosing to read
this book and listen to Sarah's story is following
the path she and her parents called
the Way of Love.*

CONTENTS

PREFACE

T HE VOICE IN THIS BOOK IS SARAH, and she speaks from the period in which she lived as a twelve year-old girl, sharing her world view, her story as she grows into a woman, and the story of her life as an adult. And yet, because time, at best, is liquid and illusionary, you will find her voice changing throughout the book as she expresses what she learns through integrating her own sense of truth and reality with the reality of her experiences in a parallel life as Pia. Through the process of integrating parallel lives, Sarah and Pia are the same energy. Pia is older and has had more experiences on Earth. Yet Sarah is wiser, having the direct experience of learning at her Grandmother's knee and from her parents when her Pleiadian family walked the Earth.

Earth is a planet that is steeped in dualistic concepts, and topics discussed in many of the following chapters may initially seem to be polar opposites. However, through Sarah's view on how to integrate all of those opposites that seem to separate everyone into adversarial viewpoints, these words can help provide peaceful perspectives of unity.

Mary Magdalene instructed Pia to set aside thirteen days for this book to be born. In that thirteen days, Sarah told her story, which you are about to read. This book also has thirteen chapters. The energy of thirteen is supremely important because it is the energy of integration, an important Pleiadian concept offered for human evolution, and if you choose to allow it, this book can help you find your own path to integration, freedom, and peace.

As you read, you may want to allow your own beliefs to dissolve and give your heart a chance to expand in fullness. As you read chapter after chapter, you may begin to recognize or increase your recognition of a larger truth and a greater reality. Earth is very small compared to the vastness of the cosmos. As Sarah speaks about your cosmic goal, the principles of duality, religion, separation and unity, water and light, movement and sound, energy and vibration, heart and mind, soul and spirit, the processes of integration and Ascension, you will hear simple truths from a clear and fresh perspective.

Truth is always simple and deep, and Sarah uses just enough story for people to relate as she shares principles to live by for more balanced and whole lives. Like her mother, Mary Magdalene, the words that are shared are as simple and direct as possible, filled with the energy of truth for those who can see and hear it. Therefore, there are not as many words in this book as you will find in ordinary books today, although many of the concepts are repeated in multiple ways to help the reader more fully absorb them. Woven into each word is the light of truth and the love that pours through Sarah as she shares her story and her perspective with the world.

Sarah is surrounded by love and filled with teachings from her family, who demonstrate higher consciousness through daily living. Her voice can bring each of you to the place of realization of how very important you are in the world, as she shares with you how to fulfill your own mission. You are all divine sparks of light, and Sarah speaks now to fill the gaps in your understanding and to help you to remember who you truly are.

~ PIA ORLEANE, Ph.D.

INTRODUCTION

T HE CONTENTS OF THIS BOOK will hopefully reverse some of the myths that have been circulated for millennia concerning the true circumstances around Mary Magdalene and her husband Jesus of Nazareth, telling the true story of what actually happened in the Biblical era. One of the most important elements of this book is the fact that Mary Magdalene was an equal partner in both marriage and in teaching the Way of Love alongside her husband, Jesus of Nazareth.

For the first time, Sarah, the daughter of Jesus of Nazareth and Mary Magdalene is revealed in this book through her own story. What is imparted here through Sarah's story may be startling to some, while others may intuitively connect with the truth that is shared.

This marvelous book was written for a culture that is steeped in traditional beliefs which may be neither helpful nor true. Although the information contained here may be startling to some, if not controversial, it is also simultaneously intriguing and thought-provoking. You will need an open heart and an open mind to absorb this never-before offered wisdom and truth. Sarah's story is a revelatory and truthful account, containing a new version of the unaltered and actual history of the Way of Love, lived and taught by Sarah's parents, Mary Magdalene and Jesus of Nazareth.

Sarah's story dispels the myriad of myths and untruths surrounding the lives of Mary Magdalene and Jesus of Nazareth, as told by Sarah through direct channeled transmissions to Dr. Pia Orleane. As Sarah is revealed through Pia, she shares the Pleiadian perspective of the true mission of her family—Jesus of Nazareth, his mother, Mary, his wife, Mary Magdalene, and their two children, Sarah and Timaeus. Sarah gives us an inside look at their family's trials and their true purpose in coming to Earth from the Stars to help humanity evolve and grow. With continued references to the teachings of both her parents, the true Pleiadian source of the Way of Love is finally revealed.

This book brings new light and a more truthful version of what actually took place in the era when Mary Magdalene and Jesus of Nazareth were here on Earth to bring their teachings to humanity, rather than the altered facts that have been handed down for the last two thousand years to misinform and control the church's followers, causing serious misinterpretations and confused beliefs about the message of The Way of Love. This information is not simply someone's interpretation of what happened—Sarah's story is an accurate first-person description of what her parents were offering to the people of this Earth. Sarah's story told to the author is a deliberate attempt to rectify the myths and altered stories fabricated by the traditional Christian church. Her story provides an enlightened view, honestly discussed, and finally brought to light!

Sarah authenticates the true story of occurrences and dispels the accepted, modern, erroneous myth surrounding the life and death of her family. Her information not only refutes the age-old erroneous myths changed over time by those who wanted to alter the truth for their own gain, but it also brings the startling beauty and love that Mary Magdalene and Jesus of Nazareth brought here in a spiritual rather than a religious context.

This new version of Biblical history may stand the Christian community on its head because it opens a completely new view of Christ and Mary's mission and what actually occurred during their lives two thousand years ago. The Christian community may see this book as blasphemous, yet the information contained in these pages is pure, honest, and direct. Although this historical account may certainly take the Christian community by surprise, it tells the true Way of Love and is actually more believable than the myriad of myths and misunderstandings surrounding Biblical history and orthodoxy that has been handed down generation after generation.

Although much of this story will be new to many of you, hopefully it will clarify what has been purposefully changed over millennia. Read this story with an open heart and mind to finally allow the true wisdom to come to you through your heart rather than clinging to a falsified and very old myth that has colored history for so long. Through the eyes and heart of Sarah, this story will touch you deeply and may change your life forever.

~ CULLEN BAIRD SMITH, Author, Lecturer

MARY MAGDALENE'S DAUGHTER

The Story of Sarah

CHAPTER ONE

WHO AM I?

Y NAME IS SARAH. My mother is Mary Magdalen, and my father is Jesus of Nazareth. I was twelve years old when my father Ascended. It was a terrible time for us because of the torture my father was forced to endure, trying to prove to humanity that there is more to life than this third dimension, which is experienced through the dualistic opposites of pleasure and pain. His example of Ascension with his body has become a legend that unfortunately many today misunderstand or misinterpret. I will explain more as I tell my story, beginning with my experiences at age twelve. I will also be jumping between my experiences when I was twelve years old living with my family and my later life as a more mature woman, as I comment on circumstances and perspectives in your modern world. Please do not be confused by time, for it is an illusion anyway. The truth is simple, and it is represented throughout this book from all the perspectives I have experienced and from what I share with Pia in her own life experiences.

To get a sense of who I am, I will describe myself. I look more like my father than my mother. I have his light brown hair, not the beautiful, thick red hair of my mother. I am also slim, like my father, whom I love dearly. I used to walk in the fields together with my father, enjoying the beauty of the lilies in bloom. He often spoke of these lilies, explaining how even the fields of grass are dressed by Nature in beautiful lilies, and that we also are beautiful when we align with Nature and remember who we truly are. To me, lilies represent not only Nature's beauty, but also pure simplicity and truth. I have a special feeling towards lilies–both their beauty and their subtle sweet smell. I feel we are related somehow, even though I do not have exceptional beauty. I feel that we are all equally beautiful when we are living from our hearts; we are all beautiful when we shine our light. I have given you a picture of me so that you can relate to me more easily as I tell you my story.

Of course, I understand the Ascension process. We are Pleiadian, and my family had a mission to help the people of Earth learn how to love, work together in harmony, and to understand the energy that makes each person who they are. My father chose to experience the worst pain possible in our time, attempting to show others how to transcend their own pain. As I said, it was a terrible time for us. My mother and my Grandmother tried to talk him out of his choice, telling him there were other ways to demonstrate transcending pain. But he was impatient with the people's lack of awareness and evolutionary progress, and he was absolutely determined to be a living example, providing evidence of higher possibilities for all.

My mother was pregnant with my brother at the time, so she also had to demonstrate how to rise above and transcend the emotional pain she was feeling from temporarily separating from my father and watching him suffer while he attempted to demonstrate rising above his physical pain. It was a hard time for my mother, being with child and knowing that my father was leaving her with the responsibility now on her own of carrying on their joint mission of teaching Love. As you will see later in the story, when my little brother was born she named him Timaeus. I think she chose that name to remind us all that we are outside the bounds of time.

The pull of duality and separation was great when we walked the Earth, as it is today. In what you perceive as my time on Earth, most people preferred (and still today prefer) to avoid examining what makes them unhappy or causes suffering. They do not realize their own reactions, beliefs, and choices cause or contribute to their sense of separation and fear. Then and now, people tend to blame others for how they feel and what is wrong in their lives, rather than taking responsibility to look inside themselves or make necessary changes to bring more harmony into their circumstances. The cause of such suffering, of course, is the underlying sense of isolation and separation from Source, or what some call God. But you can never be separated from Source or

God because you are part of Source. As we Pleiadians say, you are a divine spark of light.

Although my mother and my father worked together to bring enlightened consciousness and the Way of Love into the world in my time, my father took the lead in speaking to the people. At this time on Earth, it is absolutely necessary for the divine feminine to take the lead in showing the pathway to truth and higher consciousness. This is one reason for the increased interest in my mother's teachings, which were blatantly ignored or dismissed by most people in our own time. When I was on Earth, it was my father who proclaimed, "I am the way, the truth, and the light," following his mission to teach by example. But make no mistake—my mother and father were equals who came to this planet together in unity to teach the Way of Love. You will find many references to my father's teachings, but male energy was more dominant then; you will find more subtle (and perhaps more even more powerful) references to Love and conscious living from my mother throughout this book. I will weave them into every chapter, for like my mother, I am bringing forth messages of Love through divine feminine guidance today, even though I am not embodied as a human at this time. Merging with Pia's heart allows me to do this.

My father's light radiated unconditional Love to all, as he worked to show people how to heal. He would stand before them or touch them, reflecting unconditional Love from his heart and eyes into theirs, empowering them to find the highest aspects of who they were. When their hearts opened and they were able to become unconditionally loving, they could heal themselves, like my mother's brother, Lazarus, whom people believed to be dead, so immobile was he from his fear and imbalance. Through my father's eyes and unconditional love, he saw himself differently and began to live a new life lead by Love. Sadly, most people do not understand how that works. In my time, they believed father was healing them, rather than seeing that they were healing themselves just by feeling the effects of his unconditional Love and opening their own hearts to become unconditionally loving themselves.

Mother has always been a shining example of passion for justice, truth, endurance, transition through challenges, inspiration to others, and unconditional Love for all, in her time and now. She taught me that I, too, could teach by example through how I lived my life and the responsible, conscious choices I made. When I was twelve, I truly hoped to be like Mother when I was grown, and perhaps I achieved that, although maybe not in the way I had hoped. At twelve, I deeply longed to be able to attend the Magdalen School in Egypt when I was older like Mother did! It was there that she received her name, Mary Magdalene, which means, of course, Mary of the Magdalene Order, a high, high honor indicating cosmic understanding that is born of Love and compassion.

Every day Mother taught me to be responsible for my thoughts, my tones in speech, and my actions because they are all energy, and energy can manifest positively or negatively. Father always showed me how positive thoughts and trust could support healing or rebalancing in any person or situation. He always told people not to judge each other, but to love and accept each other unconditionally. But I saw then and throughout my life that people judged each other because they were not content within themselves. Judgment comes from within and then extends outwards. When father spoke, a sense of calm radiated from his voice and from his physical presence, too. I loved to listen to his teaching stories! He made the simple truth so easy to understand. He taught peace through unconditional Love, the way Grandmother Mary did. Mother was a bit more fiery, always speaking out for justice, but with compassion and strength and always without judgment, for unconditional Love does not judge. She simply and clearly expressed the truth, while still loving everything and everyone, whether they could see and accept the truth or not. Although often subtle, mother's teachings were always simple and deep.

While both my parents were Pleiadian, my precious Grandmother Mary, my father's mother who is known today as Mother Mary, carried both Pleiadian and angelic, energy so I carry both angelic and Pleiadian energies in who I am. Perhaps it was the strong Love and influence of sitting at my Grandmother's feet, learning while we performed our daily tasks that caused me to relate to the angelic kingdom so strongly. I think Pleiadians and angels are not so very different. Both Pleiadian and angelic kingdoms value Love as the strongest, most important force in the universe, so perhaps there is not much difference in what makes a Pleiadian a Pleiadian or an angel an angel. I don't know. All I know is that I am at peace when I am feeling compassion and unconditional Love for everyone and everything.

When I was around Grandmother Mary, I always smelled roses. The smell opened my heart to Love and made me feel grateful. I felt happy around the smell of roses, the way I felt happy when I sat at her feet as she taught me. Even today when her energetic presence is noticed, you can smell roses in the air. Learning from Grandmother Mary was beautiful. She taught me how to weave a basket or sew a garment, while telling me about Love and its power. Always the lesson centered around Love and how true unconditional Love can heal anything. But to experience that, you have to become it. You have to drop all judgment of others, even when they hurt you because they are unconscious. You also have to become unconditionally loving to all life if you want to heal imbalances within yourself. Nobody can heal another person, for the healing occurs within you when you reach a state of complete non-judgment and unconditional Love. I know that from listening to my father and because my Grandmother has demonstrated that for me over and over again in my life. I also watched my Father and Mother do the same thing in the way they lived their lives together.

When Mother was around, I always smelled Jasmine, and her smell is often present today for those who notice when her energy is around. Jasmine is a sweet, comforting smell that brings a sense of peace and calm. I don't know if this scent is special only to Mother, or if it is part of being a Magdalene, but I know that I always trusted the pure goodness of this scent. When Jasmine blooms on Earth and gives its gift of sweet scent, there is harmony and balance in the air. When I smelled Jasmine, the peace in my heart told me that there was nothing I needed to do. I needed to just be and allow the Love in my presence to bring a sense of peace as an example for others, like my mother did, like my father did, like my Grandmother did. They were brilliant examples for all who could (or wanted to) see the truth, and their examples are still inspiring today when people live in the Way of Love. I, too, endeavored to be an example of light, shining the way for others to see through the darkness. And I called on my connection to lilies to remind me that beauty can always be found in simple truth, and that we should always align ourselves with the truth that lives in Nature and in our hearts.

I have been told that there is not so much darkness where I am really from, where Mother and Father and Grandmother Mary are from, and that the darkness in the outer universe is peaceful, not disharmonious as it can be here on Earth in duality. But unlike Grandmother Mary, Mother, and Father, all I remembered for many, many years and know now is that although there is goodness everywhere here on this planet, people can't see it. All they can see is what troubles or challenges them because that is where they focus their attention. They rarely see that they create their own obstacles and struggles through their beliefs, their choices, their actions, and how they react rather than respond to others or to circumstances. They rarely take responsibility for how they judge one another, accusing others of being wrong, or how they blame others for things that they can and should correct within themselves or in their own lives through making better choices.

I return to my thoughts about how I experienced the world through scent. I was curious about the smells I sensed at age twelve. I understood the scents from the divine feminine essences of Love, for those are the fragrances I noticed when Mother and Grandmother Mary were around. But I did not understand clearly the scents around the divine masculine until I was much older. I just knew that everything had a scent, just like it had a feel, a color, a look, or a sound. At twelve, I still did not know what all scents represented, but I could tell whether they were uplifting or repelling. I liked the smell of clary sage, for it seemed healing. And juniper and the smells of all the trees expanded me. And I could not forget the subtle, sweet smell of purity I experienced around lilies, which were so important to me. But at twelve, I was still exploring this world where I walked, and I often took my many questions to Grandmother Mary.

What I knew so far at twelve, is that scents conveyed the polarity of energy; some were pleasant and very highly positive in vibration, and some were unpleasant or even offensive and conveyed a low negative vibration. This is similar to what we see and what we hear; what we smell gives us clues about the energy we are experiencing. It is one of the many guidelines we have to align ourselves with higher frequencies and move away from those that are lower in vibration. Most people do that instinctively when they experience a particular scent, but I find that conscious exploration of the energy of a fragrance can provide more useful information about how to either engage or disengage with it in an appropriate manner. I did not know what my own energetic scent was at twelve, but I suspected it had to do with the lilies I loved, and certainly that awareness and recognition of energetic alignment increased as I grew older. Now I will go back to my story.

My father had moved into the energetic realms, leaving his Earthly family to continue the work he and my mother came here to do. As soon as realistically possible for the mother of a newborn infant, Mother left on her journey to bring the teachings of Love into the world. Even while she was still at home tending to Timaeus, she was pondering how she would share the messages she was now alone responsible for communicating. As you can see from the teachings that are her legacy today, she realized that the first thing she needed to teach humanity was not to be afraid, for fear is the opposite of Love and the basis of separation. And so, she formulated her messages to be as simple as possible so that people could easily understand them. She also chose to demonstrate living on this planet in Love and how to move away from any tendency toward fear (which was planted by those who were lost in darkness) through her own choices, always moving toward the state of blissful, accepting, unconditional Love. When speaking with others, her first and last words then were often, "Fear Not!" She still uses those words when communicating with those who can hear her today—"Fear Not!"

Once Mother left on her teaching journey, Timaeus was left with my Grandmother and me to raise, as I was old enough to help with that task, and although resistant at first as you will see, ultimately, I was glad to do so. My Grandmother Mary guided me through this family challenge and transition. Like my mother, she wanted my father to choose another path of teaching by example, but as I said, he was determined to use his actions as an example for others to see and learn. So, my Grandmother, my mother, and I had to demonstrate surrender and acceptance, which leads to the grace that eases pain. My father said to the people, "The truth will set you free. But first it will test you to the limit." And my family was severely tested. We got through these tests by following my mother's teaching, "The secret of this test is to Love it all." You will find references to this core teaching throughout this book. The truth did indeed test us, tying us together as a family unit to demonstrate all the Pleiadian principles we had come to share with the world through how we lived and demonstrated unconditional Love.

So, who am I? I am Sarah, daughter of Mary Magdalen and Jesus of Nazareth, my Pleiadian parents, and Granddaughter of Mother Mary, who is part Pleiadian and part angelic. I am here to share what I have learned from my family with all on Earth who have an ear to hear and are willing to listen as you open your hearts.

CHAPTER TWO

THE COSMIC GOAL

I DIDN'T THINK MUCH ABOUT MY PURPOSE or why I was here when I was a child, but I carefully watched my parents and listened to what they told me about having a purpose. They explained to me that my purpose right now was to simply be the absolute best person I could be. Sitting at Grandmother Mary's feet every day helped me to achieve that, for she was a gentle guide who compassionately pointed out how I could, perhaps, do or say things in another way, perhaps more gently or with more compassion. Sometimes she weaved her lessons into stories, asking me what I thought the characters should do or what choices should they make?

When I was living on Earth, I never heard people ask the question, "What is my mission?" or "What is my purpose?" although perhaps they should have. And yet now as I am in an energetic form and merging my consciousness more and more with Pia, every day I hear people asking that question of Pia and her beloved Cullen. Pia and Cullen share the same heart and have the same worldview and understanding of unconditional Love, like my parents did, so it is not surprising that people ask for their guidance. It seems to me that today more people are asking that question than before, which is a good sign that consciousness, at least in some people, is rising to a higher level beyond the simple needs of daily existence on Earth.

I will address the cosmic goal that has been explained to me by Grandmother Mary and was demonstrated to me daily by my mother, my father, and my grandmother. Perhaps this will give you a deeper recognition of your purpose or mission so that you, too, can succeed in raising your conscious awareness in service to your own evolution and that of others.

The cosmic goal for this planet, Earth, and the people of this planet is to evolve into a higher state of consciousness. However, consciousness is not necessarily what you perceive it to be. It is not something that is contained in your mind, nor does it exist simply because of what you think, although the vibration of your thoughts is very important. It is not your experience of a physical reality in this plane of existence either. However, consciousness does exist in every cell of your human body, in every thought, and the choices you make determine whether your consciousness evolves or whether it gets stuck in the denseness of your current physical form. Most of you, if not all, believe that your physical body is your essence and that without it, you do not exist. Some of you grasp the idea that your awareness will continue when you no longer have a physical body (you call that death), but you are unsure what that really is. Your beliefs define that existence as heaven, the afterlife, reincarnation, or many other concepts that your minds have produced. Even with all these beliefs that you hold so dearly, you are still afraid to let your body go because it represents your consciousness to you.

When I say that consciousness exists in every cell of your body, I am trying to explain that your choices impact how that consciousness moves and evolves or becomes stuck, causing you to feel trapped. The more your choices come from Love and reflect consideration for the highest good for all, the more your consciousness expands beyond the experience of your physical form, and it becomes more possible to easily experience the freedom of true choice. Practicing choices that come from unconditional Love helps you to move into higher vibration and unity.

The more you make thoughtless choices or chose things that reflect selfishness or lower vibrational energy, such as killing for food or doing things that harm yourself or others, the more you become connected to your belief that your physical form is who you are. You become more attached to your physical body and you fear for its safety, believing that only your body represents who you are. With this type of choice (what I call an ignorant, non-thinking choice) the energy becomes stuck in your cells and you become more and more dense. Therefore, you feel more separation as an individual who suffers rather than experiencing yourself as an energy that is continually rising towards the higher vibrations of unity and freedom.

The cosmic goal and your mission require you to release your identity with being a separate person who must look out only for yourself or those you care for. You must realize that your individuality is part of a pattern of a greater whole and is a gift to all. This view frees you from restricting concepts and selfish choices that only reinforce your feelings of separation and loneliness.

The cosmic goal also requires that you achieve the recognition that your essence is held in what you may call an energetic light body until you Ascend into a Rainbow body, which I will explain soon. Your Rainbow body is free to manifest in any form you choose! You are here now in a physical form (like my family and I were) because your greater consciousness made the choice to have that experience. And your goal is to take that experience to its highest level through non-attachment and the understanding that manifesting a form begins from the place where consciousness lives in your light body. Your light body is the blueprint for what you manifest as a physical form, and it is the part of you that helps create a Rainbow body when you achieve a high enough vibration.

Ultimately, when you learn how to merge your light body with your current physical form, you will be able to heal your physical body, lighten its density, and form what I have been taught is called a Rainbow body. You practice that now when you surrender to unconditional Love and find balance within your heart, mind, and your current physical body, producing balanced, healing energy. A Rainbow body is a more advanced achievement of that process, for it holds all the positive, light energies that exist, and it moves in wave motion wherever it needs to be, becoming more solid when necessary and more fluid when it is time to move somewhere else. Freedom! Expansiveness! Cosmic expression! This is what my father did when he allowed his existing physical form to be "killed" but then reappeared on Earth several days later in a living, vibrant physical form. He was demonstrating the path and the power of attaining a Rainbow body, which can house a more expanded form of consciousness because it is consciousness that manifests our form.

To reach the cosmic goal of higher consciousness, you must have an open heart. You must stop judging yourself and others and have compassion for those who are ignorant or make mistakes. Remember, mistakes are a path of learning and are essential to elevating your awareness. So, if you have already learned something through your own mistakes, have compassion for those who are still learning. And if you are thinking of yourself as less than or better than someone else, recognize that in that moment you are judging, and judgment keeps you stuck and separated. Non-judgment and acceptance promote your expansive growth.

To achieve the cosmic goal, you must release the beliefs you hold so dearly about what is real and be curious about the larger reality. This is not an exercise of imagination, nor is it a new "belief" being given to you. This is simply a path of expansion and growth that opens through Love. I do not mean to sound as if I know more than you do; I have just attained a broader perspective. Throughout my life, I, too, was continually evolving. Time and time again my Grandmother showed me how to put my beliefs aside and allow the truth to emerge from my heart. This is what you, too, must do if you wish to achieve your mission. To be conscious and free from fear and pain, you must take responsibility for yourselves, your choices, and your actions or reactions. Choices determine how your life path emerges on your journey. Make conscious choices, for you are creating yourself and your life with every choice you make.

The most important thing to remember is that you are a being of Love. And as my mother, Mary Magdalene, continually reminded me, "Fear not!" Fear is the opposite of Love. I now know and understand that. If you want to achieve the cosmic goal and fulfill your mission, I would encourage you to dissolve all your fear and allow your Love to shine into the world. It is from this position that you allow your consciousness to expand to its highest level, creating a new form of a Rainbow body, which allows you to finally and fully become free.

CHAPTER THREE

THE PRINCIPLES OF DUALITY

The Christian Myth of the Garden of Eden

MY MOTHER FREQUENTLY REMINDED ME that all seeming opposites here in duality on Earth are actually one, for they all come from the same source of oneness. "Everything", she said, "is one, so you cannot truly feel separation when you see from the heart." I learned to look and listen to other perspectives to find the harmony of oneness, something my mother urged me to do whenever I felt any type of conflict or challenge.

It was not very difficult to make up my mind about what I wanted when I was a child, but I did give deep thought to what I believed, and my beliefs changed as I learned to find the truth within any situation. Apparently, this is a gift that not everyone has. I watched and began to understand how people align with things that make them feel happy or safe and avoid things that are different or frightening to them. Personally, even at twelve I was not frightened by things that were different; I was curious. I wanted to know more about how things worked so that I could understand it better. Therefore, every experience I had became an exploration of what I was feeling, thinking, and what choice I would like to make in response to my feelings and my thoughts. I was never one to act quickly, a quality I carried throughout my entire life on this planet. I realized that slow, considered thoughtful action was more beneficial and would create the highest good for all and that quick reactions based on raw feelings or unconsidered beliefs could cause a lot of pain and separation. I carefully listened and then considered (sometimes for a very long time!) how I was going to respond to what I either saw or heard.

I see that on this planet still today, all of your experiences are wrapped up in a misunderstanding of the purpose of duality and a complete misuse of the principles of duality. Duality here on Earth is intended to offer you different and opposite perspectives to help you learn and grow. It is part of the human evolutionary journey to experience and work with duality to expand your consciousness. Ideally, when you see something that is opposite to your own point of view or belief, it is intended that you fully examine that opposite view, reconsider your own beliefs, and determine if you need to make changes in how you see and relate in the world. This is the proper use of duality. However, what I see you doing is aligning with whatever position supports your own beliefs while dismissing as "wrong" anything from the opposite perspective. This is causing a split or separation in you that causes you pain and further separation.

It is not your fault that you have come to misuse duality so inappropriately. At one time you knew how to blend all of your opposite views into new and ever-changing beliefs. But then, you began to separate yourselves into groups who held the same beliefs, while rejecting others who were different. My family came to Earth to help guide you back towards unity and away from the separation you were creating, but we failed our task. You became even more engaged in misusing duality once we were gone, separating from each other because of your beliefs; stories about what my father and mother were teaching were eventually shaped and changed into a myth to serve another purpose.

The Christian myth of the Garden of Eden was created long after my father, mother, grandmother, and I had left this Earthly realm. I dislike even using the name, "Christian," for today's Christianity does not reflect the teachings of my family! It is a myth created for control rather than for growth and evolution. It does not tell the whole story, intentionally leaving out pieces that are key for humanity's understanding. The myth of Adam and Eve begins in the middle, not at the beginning. What is intentionally left out of the Christian myth is the beginning, where humanity actually lost its connection to divine Source, intuitive wisdom, and evolutionary growth—the time when Adam was partnered with Lilith, not Eve.

Lilith, Adam's first wife, was deeply connected to Nature and understood the patterns of chaos that were necessary for evolutionary change. She continually broke patterns of belief with unpredictable and vital erratic choices that inspired new thoughts and new patterns of behavior. Lilith was wild and chaotic herself, and her impulsive responses to life encouraged living in the moment, led by the energies that were inspired by her heart. She lived outside of history and time. Her heart's desire was to live in unity with Adam, moving together in response to energetic guidance as it arrived and integrating each other's opposite perspectives into a harmonic whole. But Adam found this challenging; he needed and preferred a more predictable and secure environment to make him feel safe and to plan for whatever might come "next." The focus on "next," a feature of time, not energy, caused them to move into a separation that increased as he brought more and more awareness of future and past into their present moment. Lilith found Adam's need for order and control of his environment too stifling for her, and one day she finally left with the wind. Although the chaotic energy Lilith represents will always be present offering new opportunities and choices in every moment here on Earth, Lilith herself simply could not be confined to predictable patterns and order while she was living with Adam in the Garden of Eden. That was the role of another, who was actually invented by those who wrote the myth. Here is what I can share of how the truth was lost and the Christian myth took over humanity's path.

According to the myth, Adam and Eve are named as the

first inhabitants of the Garden of Eden. In truth, as Adam focused more and more on the separations of time, he lost the memory of being whole in himself and began to look for someone outside of him to make him feel complete. This is where the Christian myth of the Garden of Eden today begins, and the myth leaves out some other very key points. First of all, the myth says that Eve was taken from Adam's rib, a part of him, yet Adam began to see Eve as someone outside of him. The unity Adam had experienced with Lilith was now forgotten. Rather than looking for paradise (or happiness) within himself, Adam began to look for paradise (or happiness) in connection with someone outside of himself, Eve. But as Father and Mother always explained to me, you can never truly love another nor can you feel complete if you are looking for Love and completion outside of yourself. You are whole as you are, and divine relationships share their wholeness with one another rather than looking for a person outside of them to complete them or provide the Love that should exist in their own hearts, for you are truly complete in your own hearts.

The telling of the Christian myth leads you further into ideas of separation and away from ideas connected to divine unity. But the deception deepens. Eve is short for Even, and Eve represents the patterns of order and balance, a huge step away from chaos and growth. Eve, or Even, represents patterns that keep you safely away from changes that you do not understand or opportunities to explore other perspectives. Following the steps of Eve to continually stay "even" closes your hearts to your intuition and separates you from the cycles of Nature. You need balance, but you also need the chaos that brings change and evolution, as represented by Lilith's energy.

Now we come to the Tree of Knowledge and the apple that Eve supposedly gave to Adam. Please notice that the myth names this powerful tree the *Tree of Knowledge*; it is not called the *Tree of Wisdom* in the myth. To understand the depth of this deception, you must realize that knowledge is based on facts and beliefs that are held in the mind, things that others discover or that you learn or believe from experiences that come from something outside of you. You then store these outside "facts" and beliefs in your mind as the truth, although they may only be true for a moment. These facts are unreliable because they do not always fit the circumstances of the present; they are based upon past experience, and they are not always (or often) relevant to you individually or to what is true in the moment. By contrast, wisdom lives in the heart; it is divine knowing that comes from inside of you, based on your ever-present cosmic connection to Source. Wisdom lives in your hearts to guide you moment-by-moment when you connect with and listen to your intuition (which is inside of you.) Wisdom is not bound by the perception of time. Knowledge is every-changing; wisdom is eternal!

In the myth, the serpent, represented as Evil (which is Live spelled backwards) gave Eve an apple. The backwards spelling of the word instills moving backwards from cosmic flow when you read the story, an intentional deception woven into the myth. The truth that is left out of the

Christian myth is that because this apple came from the Tree of Knowledge rather than the Tree of Wisdom, the apple was poison to human consciousnsess. Eating the apple is symbolic to entering into a state of fear and separation by focusing on beliefs in the mind, when you are designed to be led by the wisdom that lives in your heart. When you allow the mind to lead rather than the heart, you experience all the emotions of fear, shame, guilt, unworthiness, jealousy, anger, and anything else that is emotionally uncomfortable. After one bite of this apple, Adam and Eve's perspective changed to a different way of seeing themselves. Then they made the mistake of believing they were unworthy and ran away from the Garden of Eden. The myth defines this mistake as a "sin."

If you look up the etymology of the word sin, you will find that it means to make a mistake, as I mentioned earlier. My father taught that there is no such thing as a sinner; everyone makes mistakes in order to grow, and he taught that we are not to judge those who make mistakes but encourage their growth from what they can learn. The myth says that Adam and Eve became sinners when they ate from the Tree of Knowledge. But the reality is that their memory of who they were as divine beings connected to Source was suddenly clouded by a new belief held in their minds— a belief that they were unworthy, which came from fear. Suddenly they were ashamed of who they were and felt very guilty for having eaten this apple. They became afraid (the greatest toxin in the apple was fear), and they fled the Garden of Eden. Today the use of this Christian myth condemns its followers as "sinners" who are unworthy and teaches them that making mistakes is bad, and that they should fear being punished by God for their mistakes, which is the opposite of what my father and mother taught. The Christian religion teaches that you can be forgiven for your sins, but in truth, there is nothing to forgive, for each mistake is there to help you grow. It is simply your responsibility to learn from the mistakes you make so that you become more conscious and loving. It is through the making of mistakes that you grow. You actually learn more from your mistakes than from your successes!

I can easily see how today the myth of the Garden of Eden has led you to seek safety in order and predictability provided by sources outside of yourselves, instead of continually listening to the cosmic wisdom that lives in your own hearts and is available through your intuition. Perhaps you may want to consider if it is possible that you have not yet learned a lesson from a mistake that you made, or if the lesson has been learned and you are able to see things from a higher perspective now. It is up to you to determine how you are growing; no one else can tell you this. The choice to accept and encourage guidance from outside of yourself has actually deepened your sense of separation—from each other, from Nature, and from Source. You are living in guilt, insecurity, and fear, projecting the worst parts of yourselves on others as you defend who you believe yourself to be in your delusion. You seek to be even, like Eve, rather than embracing the chaos that Lilith brings in the wind to help you return to Nature and invite natural ways of evolutionary growth. You are discovering that safety can never be promised by a family, a society, a religion, a government, an artificial medicine, or anyone else. Safety can only be found by returning to the wisdom contained in your own hearts, where you are intuitively guided by your connection to God or Source. This is what my grandmother, my mother, and my father tried to share with the world. It is what I am sharing with you now. You are all divine. You are all part of Source. You are each part of a magnificent design!

In understanding this, if you choose to, you can peel off the shroud of Christian belief and control that has been placed over your eyes and begin to see and feel the true reality that my family has been trying to show humanity for a very long time. Perhaps now in your time you can choose to step away from following religions, governments, authorities, and especially your artificial technology that is supposed to make your lives simpler, but in fact seems to me to complicate and control you at an increasing speed. Perhaps all you really need is to return to Nature and invite the winds of change to bring the transformations that are needed. You must be brave to do this. You must be willing to use courage and face the unknown. You must be willing to reconcile with each other and surrender the focus upon your differences, embracing your similarities instead. My father always counselled to "Love your neighbor as yourself." After all, each of you has a heart that is connected to all other hearts. Each of you struggles under the illusion of being alone or feeling unworthy because of forgetting your wholeness through your disconnection from Source. If you stop trying to defend your beliefs, which are mostly imposed upon you from myths like the Garden of Eden or other religious and governmental controls, and if you stop trying to preserve who you *think* you are by clinging to old patterns of behavior that do not serve you or anyone else, you might have a future–one that arrives moment-by-moment as you connect to energy rather than time.

You are destined to return to unity as you move away from all the beliefs that you are separate from Source and from each other. Duality serves a purpose, but only if you use it correctly. I am speaking up today because energetically it feels like now is the moment for you to focus on returning to a unified view of life and create a new myth to live by. This new story, or new myth, comes singing from my heart! You must return to Nature, remembering that you are part of Nature. It is in Nature that you will find your sense of connection to everything, including Source and each other– a position that allows and encourages you to live in unity. It is in Nature that you remember who you are and embrace Lilith's chaos in your own hearts as you find your own courage and your will to grow and change in a balanced way that is not even but has waves of movement and change as you participate with each energy as it arrives. Through this new myth, you can learn to use duality properly, expel separation from your Garden, and invite each other into unity once again. Your Garden will thrive through these choices!

CHAPTER FOUR

RELIGION & TRUTH

THE ENTIRE TIME I WAS HERE as the Pleiadian daughter of Mary Magdalene and Jesus of Nazareth, religion ruled people. It never made sense to me that I had to do things a certain way or follow certain rules dictated by others. My heart was my ruler, and I followed the guidance of how I felt. And yet, I watched people around me judge others for not doing as they did. I watched them separate themselves through that judgment. And I watched the fear that arose from thinking that they may be judged if they did not follow the rules exactly. So, my earliest opinions of religion stayed with me my whole life. I find religion still negatively influences people today. True spirituality does not require religion or its rules and guidelines. Your connection to your heart and to Source provides all the guidelines you need. Let the spirituality in your heart that is directly connected to Source be your only religion, for it is true.

In my family, we practiced spirituality rather than religion. That means that we knew and honored that we were directly connected to Source; we followed our hearts; and we always tried to do the best thing in any situation, with kindness, compassion, and Love. Spirituality offers a sense of freedom that is missing in religion, which may have some spiritual ideals, but is based on sets of rules that must be rigidly adhered to. I wanted to be free, and thankfully, my mother, father, and grandmother supported that, seeing that I routinely made choices that were aligned with my heart for the highest good of everyone.

My father was frequently away from home, always teaching through his example and the stories he shared. I never really missed him when he was away teaching because the presence of his Love and support were always with me in my heart, and I understood and accepted what he was doing.

When he returned, there was so much joy from the presence of my mother and father together! Our home was filled with so much light and Love that it was clear to me that together they had a great purpose of spreading that light into the world. I simply could not be selfish and wish my father to be home more frequently. Often others came to be with my father and mother and eat supper with us, as my father shared the truth. I felt he always loved everyone present equally, turning his loving gaze on each of us and touching our hearts with his light. But for my mother, there was always a special light in his eyes, for she was part of him as his true partner on this Earth mission. The Love they radiated together blessed everyone present.

My mother taught me to view every experience as just a learning and not to have any hopes or expectations of what that experience meant or what it would bring. Therefore, I was almost always at peace and could use my emotions to create a space of peace in my heart very quickly whenever I found myself out of balance. Grandmother Mary helped me practice this, too. This way of using my emotions to learn and change kept me living fully in the present moment, paying attention and learning, rather than thinking on some future that may never exist. I was content, often even filled with gladness.

So how did humanity move away from spiritual practices, peace, and the happiness I describe to live in a way that is filled with so much suffering, separation, and a constant attempt to fulfill religious rules and rituals that do not bring peace or connection? What caused that loss of direct connection to spirit? Here is my opinion; you can align with it or dismiss it, as your heart guides you.

You just read what I think about the Christian myth of the Garden of Eden, and hopefully, I shared with you how that myth has caused you to step away from your evolutionary path of learning through the choices you make; the myth has led you to rely on others outside of you rather than relying on your own connection to God or Source.

As I have already said, what you have been taught about Christianity is false. It is the opposite of what my mother and father taught —an abomination of the truth— for it teaches that you are separate from God and that you must rely upon someone else outside of your own divine self for guidance, protection, or to connect directly with God or Source.

My father and mother would be saddened by the way their teachings about Love have been twisted by today's Christian Church in a doctrine that is more about power and control than Love. The Church that supposedly is my father's legacy and which totally spurned and denigrated my mother, seems to me to be more concerned with manipulating people in order to achieve some kind of ultimate power than about the truth and simplicity of Love, which is the source of freedom, healing, and connection. This is a travesty.

It is so sad to me that the wonderful truths shared by my parents and grandmother have been twisted to confuse and control people. The very use of the term "worship" (which is encouraged in all religions) separates you from Source, as if God is larger than you are. God cannot be larger than you, for you are a part of God. To "worship" anything is to place a higher value upon what you are worshipping than upon you yourself; it is to place another in a position of awe because that someone is assumed to be higher than you can ever be. The truth is that you can reach for the stars, just as I always did, for we are all part of the stars and Source. You, too, are energy that manifests as divine sparks of light. How you use that light is up to each of you, and you must take responsibility for using your light wisely and appropriately. Your light will always be part of you.

My father often told people to "let your light shine" or "do not hide your light under a bushel basket." When you diminish the magnificence of who you are by hiding your light or placing another (rabbi, priest, pastor, or preacher) in a higher position, you are separating yourself from Source, as well as presuming that someone else is closer to God than you can ever be. How limiting and sad! To me it seems that you are actually denying your own divinity and ignoring your responsibility to shine the light of who you truly are into the world. While it is excellent to listen to others' perspectives and what they have to share (which is the proper use of duality), it is your responsibility to weigh what you see and hear with the wisdom that lives within you. It is actually very irresponsible to simply expect others to make your decisions for you, whether those decisions be rules to live by, health decisions, or anything else. This is a planet that offers and encourages the power of choice as an opportunity for growth, but you are always responsible for your own choices. If you hold the belief that you are being told what to do, going along with whatever you are told may seem like it is not a choice. However, not making a choice is actually choosing to refuse responsibility. A very good friend of mine shared the insight an insight with Cullen, who uses it regularly today. That insight is: "It is just as divine to say No as it is to say Yes." This is a powerful and important thing for you to remember! If something feels right to you, say Yes to it. If something feels wrong to you, simply say No to it.

Saying no to the idea of worshipping something outside of you is a good thing. Saying yes to gathering with others who share your desire to evolve and grow is also a good thing. Where I lived, people gathered together to sing, enjoying how the tones and melody raised their vibrations together. Such gatherings were a celebration of joy and helped us to remember our true selves. Today it seems people have forgotten how to do that. Instead, they gather to worship or listen to someone else's interpretation of the truth through what you call a sermon. Even the songs in these gatherings are not songs of joy to raise your vibration, but instead reflect words aimed at reminding you that you are small and must rely upon a larger energy to guide and protect you. But when you listen to your own heart and join your energy with others who are singing in joy, the guidance flows to you automatically, and your higher vibrational energy keeps you safe. You don't need someone else to do that for you. Safety can always be found in your heart.

You call the place of your regular gatherings synagogues, cathedrals, or churches, but the churches you join seem to me to be vehicles of separation and control, where your similar beliefs are upheld and the beliefs of others are judged as being wrong. How can this be anything but separation? Often the lessons you are given by the leaders of these churches are messages to remind you that you are small or worthless or to prescribe things you "should" do according to someone else's rules. You are neither small nor worthless. You are large and powerful, wonderful and valuable! Each of you matters, as each of you brings light into the world. You have the truth written in your hearts, and you do not need the rules of someone else to guide you about how to live. All you need to guide you is the Love in your own hearts.

My mother and father told everyone to listen to the still small voice within them. That voice comes from your heart and your connection to God or Source. That voice will always tell you the truth, while listening to others outside of you may not reflect the truth at all. I was taught to always pay attention to that still small voice inside of myself, and I know that when I did not do that, I found myself confused and in trouble. Today many people are confused for that very reason. They try to be loyal to things or people they are told they must be loyal to, without feeling the correctness of their loyalty. This leads them to feel guilty because they cannot reconcile what they are doing that someone else has told them they should do with what their hearts are telling them to do. They are ignoring their heart's guidance to choose to do something else. This takes people away from their true essence and makes them unhappy.

Pleiadians know that the greatest loyalty and the only loyalty that really matters is loyalty to the truth. And the truth can only be found in your connection to Source through the wisdom in your heart. Lilith tried to help Adam understand that truth changes as energies and circumstances change. What is appropriate in one moment is inappropriate in another. This means loyalties change as well, and if you pay attention to being loyal to the truth your heart shares, you will not be unhappy. Chaotic change brings new opportunities, and if you cling to belief in something that is no longer real, you are going to have a conflict in your heart. You must be open to what is happening right now and act according to the guidance of the moment. That is being loyal to the truth and living authentically– one of the first cosmic (not religious) rules to live by. No religion or set of religious rules can tell you what is true. But listening to your heart will always tell you what is true. There are certain cosmic truths that are eternal. I will list a few of them here, but you must recognize that these are not rules per se, they are things that your heart simply knows are always true.

1. **Do no harm**. This means not thinking or acting in a harmful way toward yourself, anyone else, any animal, plant, or the planet itself. It does not mean that you can kill some animals or some people for your own purposes but not others. Your heart hurts when you harm another, and it hinders your evolution.

2. **Love your neighbor as yourself.** This is a principle of unity. It helps you to understand that when you separate yourself from another, both you and the other feel the pain of that separation. When you accept others as they are, you are acting in the spirit of unity.

3. **Do not judge others.** Non-judgment encourages acceptance, compassion, and connection with others, which is another step towards unity and away from separation.

4. Help others when appropriate, but always take responsibility only for yourself. It is never your job to change someone else or to accept their responsibility for them. The only person you can change is you, and your only responsibility on this planet is to be the best person you can be and evolve into higher and higher states of awareness.

Many people are waiting for my father to return to Earth as he did before. But he will not revisit the people of Earth in human form. He and my mother are already here in their Pleiadian energetic forms. While my mother is the voice of wisdom of the divine feminine, spoken through many who connect with her energy, my father chooses not to speak through humans at this time. He has stepped back from the humans who insisted he was God rather than understanding that the phrase "son of God" was meant to show humanity how you are all "sons" (or "Suns"—divine light) of Source.

The world in which you currently live is even more unbalanced than when my family and I walked this planet. You are desperately in need of the divine feminine energy and a return to honoring Nature. Therefore, my parents and the council of Pleiadian Elders have now given my mother the role of bringing the wisdom of the Christ light and the Way of Love forth in the current energies. It is her voice that contains the needed nurturance, power, and truth that need to be heard, and it is at her insistence that I, her daughter, dictated to Pia this small book to reveal the truth and to help humanity move beyond your false beliefs and reliance upon organizations that foster control and separation, like your current religions and governments.

Even when I was only twelve years old, I could see that to agree to or accept anything that did not support one's own evolution was harmful to all. You are not wrong if you step away from churches, cathedrals, or synagogues that are dripping in gold while people are starving. You are not wrong if you step away from those who belittle you and label you as a "sinner," which remember, simply means one who makes mistakes and is learning. You are not wrong to step away from principles that teach that God can only be experienced by certain special people (rabbis, priests, ministers, preachers) in a prescribed way, judging everyone else to be wrong. And above all, you are not wrong to step away from the fear that you will not be loved if you see the truth and respond from your heart. You will never be wrong if you simply listen to and rely upon your heart to lead you.

My Grandmother Mary would suggest that you put down your beliefs that you are small and must rely upon someone greater outside of you, for there is no one greater than you are. You are great! And in your greatness, it is your responsibility to listen to your heart, not to a set of rules written long ago and corrupted from their original meaning. Grandmother Mary would say have the courage to set aside all the things you have been "told" are true and quiet your mind. Have the courage to listen to your heart and to let your light shine. Have the courage to love everything without judgment and to be part of the God that you are. My father and mother would remind you to spend time in Nature, for Nature always reminds you of the sacredness of life and your connection to everything.

I encourage you to make good choices. This is a planet of choice, and it is through higher choices that you can achieve the cosmic goal to evolve into a state of higher consciousness. My mother works now with a modern group of Pleiadians on Earth named Laarkmaa. Both she and Laarkmaa use Pia's voice (and Cullen's heart and mind joined with Pia's) to bring forth the words people need to hear today. In fact, Pia and Cullen must be touching for this new Pleiadian group called Laarkmaa to voice their perspective through Pia's voice. Laarkmaa has outlined guidelines of choices that live in everyone's hearts. It is up to you to make these choices or not. I will list them here[1]:

1 – Choose Love;

2 – Chose trust;

*3 – Choose to create new perspectives
    for cooperation rather than competition;*

4 – Choose to be compassionate;

5 – Choose transcendence;

6 – Choose truth;

7 – Choose to illuminate your lives with joy!

8 – Choose to connect;

9 – Choose harmony;

*10 – Choose to be aware, to be responsible,
     and to make choices from the heart in
     every present moment.*

Above all, be loyal to the truth that lives in your heart, for it contains all the wisdom of these ten choices. The truth in your heart reminds you that you are a divine spark of light directly connected to Source!

. . . .

Note 1: These choices are taken from the book ***Remembering Who We Are–Laarkmaa's Guidance on Healing the Human Condition***; Pia Orleane, Ph.D. and Cullen Baird Smith; Onewater Press, Santa Fe, New Mexico; 2015.

CHAPTER FIVE

SEPARATION & UNITY

I N MY TWELFTH YEAR OF LIFE on this planet, my world was turned upside down. I lost my father, and soon after, I lost my mother. Or at least that was what I believed at the time. However, that was not the truth. My mother simply left to go to France to continue the teachings of Love as she and my father had promised to do. It only felt like I lost her because I was more focused on the loss I experienced that felt wrong to me than on the reality of what was actually happening, which was right for everyone. My father had surrendered himself to the political authorities, in hopes of helping them see a larger reality. As everyone knows today, he was killed for that attempt to be of service to humanity. Soon after that terrible loss, my mother began to prepare to leave our home as well, which was a dreadful prospect for me. I felt alone, even though Grandmother Mary was with me and promised we would be together. I was shaken. I was afraid. And I was sad, very, very sad.

With Grandmother Mary's help, I soon learned more fully what caused my sense of separation and how to find again what I perceived to be lost through clearer perceptions of the larger truth, which returned me to a state of unity. I had not truly lost the Love of either my father or my mother. Their energy was all around me. What I perceived as the time of our deepest separation actually taught me how to always return to unity. That may sound strange, but it is in our recognition of the importance of unity that we feel the pain of separation the most. Unity lives in our hearts; it is part of our natural connection to Source. Beliefs and unbalanced choices can cause separation, which is painful because it is unnatural and illusionary.

It was during this time that my mother was pregnant with my little brother and making her plans. Mother knew the baby was a boy, and given the political challenges of our time, this made the forthcoming arrival of a baby boy even more dangerous for our family. My father and mother discussed how to keep the family safe and how to carry on the Pleiadian teachings they had promised to share with humanity. Their discussions had continued even after the government had separated my father from our family physically, first by imprisoning him, then later torturing and killing him. Father and Mother continued their communications telepathically, as they decided together how my mother would proceed when he was no longer here in the physical. We all knew that he was going Home but that he would also simultaneously be with us energetically and with his Love. Through the energy of Love, we were always connected in unity.

And then my father Ascended before returning to Earth in Rainbow body form. I quickly learned to connect with him after he Ascended; I simply saw his energy without his physical form and could feel his Love. He was there for me. He was there for my mother. When he returned in Rainbow body form, we were ready because we already knew and accepted the principles that allow Ascension with the body, and we trusted that he would return to us, at least for a short while before returning to his place in the stars.

My mother was now committed to continue teaching the Way of Love on Earth, and for this, she had to leave the land that had persecuted my father. As a girl, I would not be watched very closely. But a boy would have to be protected and kept safe. Mother also knew that a new baby would not feel safe and content traveling with her; babies need stability. So she decided to leave my little brother with Grandmother Mary and me for his own wellbeing. She waited until the impending birth and a time of nursing the new baby and strengthening herself had passed before she left to go to France, where she felt energetically drawn. My uncle agreed to help her with her travels, and also to help us whenever we needed it. Although I wanted to go with Mother, it was settled; I was to stay behind with Grandmother Mary and help to care for the new baby, at least for now.

And so, when Mother departed for France with my uncle, I was left at home with Grandmother Mary and my new baby brother, Timaeus. One of the greatest lessons Grandmother Mary ever taught me was how to find what is lost by realizing that it is never really lost because all things are connected and exist in every moment. I came to understand that all we have to do is to realize that changing our perspective can help us feel more connected. We can ask the universe to show us how to connect with what or who we feel we have lost and help us bring them back into our conscious awareness. That is how we find and recover what is lost. That is how I learned to find the sense of unity when I felt the separation caused by the seeming loss of my father, and then my mother, too.

This is what Grandmother Mary did for our family at the time of our greatest trouble. She was a great support for my mother, who sorely missed the presence of her husband during her pregnancy and after the birth. Because of political dangers and opinions, Mother could not let it be known that she was carrying the child of my controversial father. Likewise, I was hidden away, even though girls held much less importance to the government than boys. I was not a threat, but I was hidden away for safety anyway.

Day after day I sat at my Grandmother's feet doing tasks that kept my mind and fingers busy, while my Grandmother would sing or tell me stories to uplift my spirits. She told me how we can feel the energy of another even when they are at a distance, proving that there is really no separation. The idea of distance is something that only exists in this third dimensional plane, but in the true reality, we are never really separated at all. I learned to see both my father and my mother when they were not with me physically.

On a dualistic planet, separation and unity are at opposite poles of understanding. I find that separation, although it can be physical, is a thing of the mind, while unity is a connection through the heart. If you love someone, you are always connected and they are never lost to you, even when not physically present. This concept can be of great comfort to people when they "lose" someone through death. Understanding that they are not really lost, but that their energy has simply changed form, helps you to offer Love and support for the next stage of their journey until you find them again. I mention this because most of you have not yet learned how to achieve the process of Ascension, which I will discuss later, and you still experience a sense of loss when someone moves on through death. Most people today still go through the process of losing others through death and through the dying process themselves. I would venture to say from what I have seen around me, that when people die, they very quickly understand that they are returning to a state of unity and that the pain of separation felt on this planet is no longer a part of their experience. And yet those left behind cling to their sense of loss and separation because of their belief systems and their inability to accept that there has simply been an energetic change of form. Being in Nature can help open your perceptions to the larger reality and adjust to the energetic changes that occur when someone you love has gone through that transformative process. When you are spiritually aligned with Source, which is easy to do in Nature, you can align energetically, too, and healing of pain, connection with loved ones, and a return to balance is possible.

Proper use of duality can help you understand that separation is always a perception of experience used to reach a greater understanding of true unity. As previously explained, when you can see and accept perspectives that are opposite (or separate) from your own and integrate them into your own perspectives, you create unity even while seeing and experiencing the separation that appears to exist. This also applies to simultaneously experiencing a temporary sense of separation from a loved one who has died and the understanding that you are always connected in your hearts!

I close this chapter by encouraging you to always strive for unity in your choices so that you do not feel the pain of separation. Remember the Pleiadian understanding my mother shared: "Darkness is actually part of the light in oneness; it has just lost its way." Therefore, when you see darkness, be compassionate with others rather than judging them. Work to incorporate their dualistic beliefs into your own belief system for a larger perspective. And above all, let go of your fear of what is different, for when you release your fear, you will find the unity of Love and joy. Fear is only a concept of the mind; it never exists within your heart.

CHAPTER SIX

WATER & LIGHT

I T WAS OBVIOUS from the first few moments of his life that my little brother Timaeus remembered that he was Pleiadian. He had a deep interest in the stars and light, and as an infant, he gazed intensely at the stars in the night sky. Grandmother Mary and I learned that the quickest way to soothe him when he was distressed was to walk him under the stars. Even in daylight, he was always happier when outside in the light.

When Timaeus was still a baby, I took him to play in the water every day. We had a little stream near our house, with some rushes that grew on the sides, so we could safely play and not be seen by others. We could sit and put our feet in the stream or we could venture out a little way and play in the water and not be seen by curious eyes. The water was always refreshing, and it was a joy to play there. Timaeus would laugh as I splashed water onto his tiny body. He grew up loving water, as I did, and learning about its many properties from our shared experiences.

Pleiadians know that water is magic because it holds the properties of fluidity, changeability, cleansing, transporting, connection, and communication. It can be in multiple states of manifestation, according to outer circumstances and need: liquid, solid, gas, or even etheric. Water knows how to flow over, under, around, or through obstacles. It knows how and where to move. It changes state according to what is most appropriate in any given situation. Water cleanses anything that is not in harmony, whether that is something dirty, like your hands or your clothes, or whether that is something inside of you that needs to be changed; being in the water can cleanse your emotions, your attitudes, and your thoughts. It is a change-maker. Water transports information and material. It transports information from cell to cell in your bodies; it is responsible for making the blood and plasma that move through your bodies; it transports material from one place to another. And it can transport you into another state of being, if you surrender to its magic.

Water also connects you. My mother always said that waves of water are related to waves of light (a Pleiadian understanding), and we were here to help people recognize and remember their own light. Here on this planet, you are primarily made of water, and like the water of the sea, each drop that makes you human contributes to the whole sea of humanity in unity. Because of the wisdom that water carries, you can also communicate to each other through water. It is the water in the air that carries your thoughts telepathically to another person, not the air itself. It is the water that receives telepathic messages from others. It is because you are water that you have that gift of magically communicating with each other without words. Remember that you are water beings with all of water's properties.

You are taught that as humans you were made from Earth and that you return to Earth when you die. I have a different opinion. I know that you are made mostly of water, and that when you Ascend, it is the water that causes that transition to occur. It is the water that moves you from one state of being to another, changing from the liquid water in your blood and the solid water in your bones to the etheric water that holds the essence of your consciousness.

Waves of energy are like waves of water. All energy is fluid, changeable, connective, communicates a vibratory message, and can transport you from one state to another. So here on Earth, paying attention to the properties of water teaches you about the energy of being a cosmic citizen in the universe. This is the most important reason for learning about energy and vibration, which I will discuss a bit later. Meanwhile, learning to honor the water that you are, the water of others, and the water of the planet speeds your understanding of life and evolution.

Light is the other element that makes you who you are. You are a human being made of water who comes from the light of the stars, so you carry both water and light in your makeup. This is what makes you a divine spark of light. You can use the light that you are to see how you are honoring or polluting the water of your body. What choices do you make? Do you wish a clean and vibrant body by choosing pure and healthy foods, good thoughts, and good deeds? Or do you abandon your responsibility to choose wisely, allowing the water of your body to become stagnant and polluted, thereby dimming your light? Light is strongest when it radiates outwards; water is most powerful when it flows.

From the Pleiadian perspective, the above questions are important questions, because we see that light equates to Love. When your light shines brightly, your Love can be seen and felt by others. When your light is dulled through poor choices and actions, you cannot achieve the cosmic goal of higher consciousness. Unconditional Love is radiated through the light you are able to shine when making conscious, positive choices.

My father told stories about times when lions lay peacefully beside lambs. That story reflects the way animals in Nature used to behave before humans began killing for food. Today in your world animals also kill for food. When you raise your consciousness to recognize that killing in any form is a lower vibrational choice, and that you simply cannot nurture your body by eating something that comes from the lower vibration of killing, your consciousness grows. In reaching this understanding and acting upon it, you will make a major evolutionary leap towards peace. Wars on this planet will stop because people will automatically make choices for the highest good of all in unity and stop fighting and killing because of perceived separation. And animals that have killed to eat will change their patterns of behavior as well because the energy of the planet will change. You can already see this happening. As more and more people eat plant-based diets, you also see more and more examples of animals that typically fight with each other suddenly co-existing peacefully together in what you may call a peaceable kingdom.

You actually nurture yourself with foods that are infused with light and Love, the highest vibration. Plants give you all the gifts you need to nurture your bodies, and in eating a diet that entirely comes from the gifts of the plants on this planet, you fill yourself with more light! My family understood this and ate a diet that did not involve killing or violence in any form. The group known as the Essenes knew this and practiced it during my family's time on Earth.

While my father respected the choices in diet of those who still believed that they must eat fish or other animals, in our house, only living, light-filled foods were eaten. We always invited others to share our meals, if they chose, and often our tables were full with other people who came to experience the light-filled food and unconditional Love that was always present in our family and at our table. Meal time was a time of connection and sharing, and I always learned something interesting by quietly listening to what the adults were discussing. In other words, I took in the energy of the conversation as well as the energy of the meal. This is an important recognition that I think needs to be mentioned because so many of you today take in negative energy through discussing problems, watching or listening to negative things on your televisions or computers during meals, or simply rushing to eat rather than slowing down enough to express gratitude for the gift of the food you are eating. It doesn't make sense to me to be eating while you are doing something else because eating is a sacred opportunity to honor and nourish your physical body, your mind, and even your spirit. The more light you invite into yourself, the more quickly you achieve your cosmic goal, so ask yourself this question: " Is it more important to rush while I am eating or to slow down and invite more light into my body as I eat?" I think the answer is obvious.

I want to emphasize that water and light are essential qualities that make up who you are. And it is up to you to take responsibility for caring for both your inner light and your body's water. As my mother often said, "You are all sparks of divine light." And as humans on Earth, you are primarily made of water. Never forget that water is a divine feminine element, teaching how each of you can flow over, around, or through obstacles, dissolving them through your Love and changing your perspectives for a more harmonious life.

Remember that I said water made Timaeus laugh as a baby? Well, I also always laughed when around water; it brought me joy! And I loved watching the play of light on the water. The happiness of being in water and understanding the magic and gifts that water brings always gave me immediate joy that burst into spontaneous laughter! Try it sometime; surrender to the wisdom of the water and remember that you are water too, therefore, you also contain the element of magic!

CHAPTER SEVEN

MOVEMENT & SOUND

MY MOTHER REPEATEDLY EXPLAINED to me that every experience holds possibilities for learning and possibilities for positive change. I mention this to you in your now moment, knowing that you still view many things as being in the past or the future even though your possibilities for positive change are always in the present moment. I had to learn this, too. As I speak today, I will be jumping between my historical experience as a child and my perspective as an adult who had learned much. I will begin with an example that comes from my adult perspective, although I began learning this from watching my baby brother grow.

There is nothing more instructive than watching a baby or a child grow from their place of innocence through learning the consequences of what they do and how they choose to be in the world. Every choice a child makes teaches her or him a lesson and begins a pattern of belief about reality. This is why it is important to guide children to pay attention to the choices they make and learn to recognize that they can change what they are choosing at any time. Each now moment can bring positive change! This is important for adults, too. In other words, once a choice is recognized as being incorrect, the action can be stopped, and the child or adult can make another choice. All choices have consequences, but making a different choice in the now moment can alter the consequences of what was previously begun if caught and changed quickly enough. And if not caught immediately, the consequences can be transcended through responding appropriately to the challenge that has been created. It requires conscious attention, which is something Grandmother Mary showed me when I was too small for words. I watched, and I learned. Both as a child and as an adult, I paid attention to everything I thought, felt, and did, and I felt quite happy because I usually found my choices resonated with my heart and helped me to feel peaceful no matter what was going on around me. I strived to show Timaeus the same thing when he was young so that he learned to make conscious choices also and could always find peace in his heart.

Movement (a choice of action) and stillness (a choice of inaction) are very interesting to view, both in ourselves and in others. Timaeus was a quiet but curious child. Watching how he navigated between curious activity and being very, very still as he was taking something in to better understand it was very instructive for me.

Humans typically see movement and stillness as complete opposites, and I was no different in how I understood the concept of either being very still or moving around when I was young. Those two things seemed so different, and yet when I looked closer, I realized that movement and stillness were just another example of how things that are seemingly separate and opposite are actually unified in harmony. They are two sides of the same coin. Pleiadians are aware that there is always movement in stillness and always stillness in movement. Every still moment contains the potential of the next movement. Every movement has the potential for coming to rest in stillness. These potentials are seed points of energy that are real and alive. With that understanding, I could easily sense when Timaeus was about to move before he actually did—the potential movement was held within his stillness. Dolphins are aware in this way also; they, too, can sense when movement is about to occur in another dolphin or human before the movement actually takes place. They anticipate the movement in the stillness before it occurs. The apparent oppositeness of stillness and movement provide a harmonious rhythm of change and growth interwoven with periods of rest, regeneration, and preparation for the next movement, whenever it is appropriate. An example of this interchange is easily visible when you watch the relationship between the in-breath and the out-breath when you breathe. There is stillness between the movement of the two breaths. This rhythm of potential between stillness and movement is inherent in all experiences.

Everything in the universe is either moving or preparing to move because change is the nature of evolution. People try to keep things the same because they feel safe if things are the same and predictable. They know what to expect, even if it is unpleasant. But constantly focusing on the familiar to feel safe does not allow change that the unfamiliar provides to stimulate growth and evolution and which may bring even better circumstances! Grandmother Mary showed me how I could always feel safe by returning to the calm feeling of Love in my heart in any moment and in any circumstance. I want to share with you that if you remove your emotional reaction to what is unfamiliar and simply become curious about what is occurring, you also can find the safety you need through trusting in the universe, Source, and your own inner guidance. You will always know how to respond, and it is that inner knowing that keeps you safe.

In my life, creating specific times for rest was a part of every day, for my family knew and understood that the seed of potential movement was strengthened by resting and regenerating while that seed grew and prepared to sprout. We meditated in the quiet first thing in the morning, sometimes together and sometimes alone, and then we began the day's work. After lunch we rested again, the seed of inactivity and rest having been planted and grown during the meal just eaten, which provided our bodies nourishment. In the resting period, the seed of movement began to grow again until it was time to finish the day's activities. This is how we harmoniously lived in the cycles of movement and stillness.

I also learned about the power of sound by watching how Timaeus responded to all sounds. Timaeus automatically contracted in his little body as an infant when he heard an irritating tone or some other disturbing sound. I would soothe him with a song and watch as my sounds of peaceful tones and happy music created the space for him to expand into himself comfortably again. He provided a living example for me of how powerful sound is in its manifestation of form. When he was still a child and someone used harsh words against him or criticized him for making a mistake, Timaeus would always come to me for soothing his energy back into harmony. He learned how to do this for himself as he grew older, often humming or singing to dispel a negative or unpleasant sound, whether it was from something someone had said or something else in his outside environment.

My father and mother had explained to me that sound is the initiating point of creation. It is through sound that everything is created. I believe it was written down erroneously in your Bible that "In the beginning was the word." But that is an incorrect and limited version of how things actually work, interpreted by people who were not fully aware of how *all* sound manifests reality—not just words. So many things were recorded incorrectly or incompletely. This is why I am writing this book now, to help you understand the deeper levels of truth and how things really happen, for many simple truths have been altered over the years through misunderstanding or incorrect beliefs that you simply accept as normal or the truth.

It should be recognized that sound impacts everything, for it is a vibration that you can actually feel. When the Earth moves in an Earthquake, you can hear the potential in the stillness before the movement actually begins. When you speak to another, your first tone impacts them before they react or respond to the words and tones you use. It is the vibration that invites or repels interaction and connection. Words of kindness encourage high vibrational response and connection. Harsh tones or words full of judgment and criticism encourage low vibrational reactions and separation. It is a very simple concept, but one that is not as well understood by people today as my family understood it. We were always careful of the tones we used and how we spoke our words to others.

Both Timaeus and I understood the Pleiadian concept taught by my parents that "we speak each other into being," and we consciously chose both to use positive words and tones when communicating and to dispel anything we heard that did not reflect the higher aspects of who we were. When we were both grown, we realized how much honoring that principle had shaped who we were and how we could positively influence shaping others into their own highest versions through using kind tones and words when we spoke to them. Timaeus used this information to help others understand the power of sound related to place also, teaching others to listen to the sounds that were present in any place to understand what its energy had to say. Many frequent discordant sounds in a particular place create a discordant energy that underlies and affects everything else that occurs in that space. All spaces hold either harmonious or discordant energy long after they are produced. Negative tones or energy discourage you from staying in a particular place. Harmonious sounds like birdsong or wind in the trees or water rippling over stones create a peaceful environment that invites you to participate with the energy of such a place, providing a sense of calm and nurturance.

You can take this recognition of the power of sound and use it in your own life, making choices to live in peaceful environments rather than choosing to live in large cities or congested areas where discordant and negative sounds are so disruptive to the environment. Remember, this is a planet of choice, and do not agree to being trapped in any environment that is disharmonious to you. Make another choice. Your heart will show you how to make that choice a manifested reality. A peaceful environment will always cause you to feel better and more whole.

The flow of energies in the cosmos reflects into Earth, even though it is not very well understood here. Every silence in the universe holds the seed point of the creative power of sound, just as every stillness holds the seed point of movement. Evolution of all consciousness comes through the process of change, so the universe is always changing. Likewise, on Earth, elevation of your consciousness, the cosmic goal, is held in change and the choices you make in every moment. You are powerful beings of light who are continually manifesting your own reality, often without even realizing it. That is why conscious choices make such a difference.

As you become more conscious, you make wiser choices and manifest a better world. We tried to show you this when our family walked the Earth, but not many of you understood. I am trying to reach you now, once again, by explaining everything my mother, Mary Magdalene, and my Grandmother Mary explained to me, as well as what I learned from listening to my father. Read these words and take them into your heart, if you will. You are capable of so much more than what you normally experience. Learn to listen to the silence for the seed point of movement that is coming to help you change. Learn to pay attention to the seed point of stillness that calls you to rest and regenerate. Learn to use the sounds you make and the sounds of Nature to manifest peace in your lives.

CHAPTER EIGHT

HEART & MIND

THE HEART AND THE MIND are two parts of consciousness that should not be separate, but should work together in unity. My parents and Grandmother Mary demonstrated this for me my whole life, and I tried to set the same example for my little brother, Timaeus. I listened to my heart every minute of the day. I noticed how I felt about what I thought, what I said, and what was going on around me. Then I asked my mind to make choices based on my heart's guidance. I always instructed my mind to follow what my heart dictated.

These two precious parts of being human—heart and mind—are not meant to be separate. They are meant to work together as a team to make excellent choices! However, I notice that today, even more than when I was living on Earth, people value what their minds tell them more than what their hearts have to say. You must reach a balance between paying attention to what you feel and then carefully considering how to act for the highest good for all. Both feelings and thoughtful consideration are essential to peaceful joining of heart and mind together. This is why responding is more appropriate than reacting in any situation, for it gives you time to consider what you are feeling, to then use your emotions to show you what needs to change within you, and then finally to use your mind to make a good choice based on the heart's guidance.

Often things like money or power or perceived safety are the things the mind presents for decisions, while the heart's wisdom is completely disregarded. But in truth, the heart is not interested in power or money; it is only concerned with exchanges that are based on Love. Reversing your cultural priority of mind over heart to heart over mind will ultimately bring more flow and grace into your lives. Living in this way will always help to create a unified consciousness for your evolutionary growth.

I thought my greatest test had been given to me at age twelve when my father Ascended. However, my test of separation of heart and mind came when my mother left for France to teach and share the Way of Love, and I was left behind. I was saddened because I had already lost my father, and now my mother was leaving me, too. I felt empty and alone inside, even though I loved and enjoyed being with my Grandmother very much and understood my responsibility to care for my little brother. Still, I hurt. And because I was hurting so much, it was difficult for me to find peace in my heart or to quiet it enough to allow connection with the mind to decipher the best course for me to take. I withdrew. And I cried– a lot. I tried to hide my tears and sadness around my grandmother, although she was always caring and compassionate. She knew and understood what I was going through, and my heart knew that she could help me. But I didn't want to be helped; I wanted to hold on to my sadness without having my beliefs or perspective changed through a more positive point of view. I escaped to the water and let the tears pour down my face, feeling totally helpless and abandoned. I didn't want to be left behind. I didn't want to be strong and responsible. I wanted to feel that I was special and important enough to go with my mother for her great mission, not simply be left behind as a child. In short, I wanted to feel loved, and I had to adjust my perspective to realize just how loved I really was.

Even though I tried to hide my tears, Grandmother Mary helped me anyway, as she always helped me with everything. Quietly watching my withdrawal and my downcast expression, she would call me to her side and tell me stories, while she rocked baby Timaeus. Each story took away a little bit of my selfish perspective and my pain, opening me to feel the Love that was always present from both my parents as well as from her. Some stories explained the gift of Love I could feel from my little brother if only I allowed it, although at the time I incorrectly perceived him to be the reason I was excluded from going to France with my mother. Only later did understand just how incorrect I had been.

During this time, I learned a lesson about perfection, something I had never really considered before, but I was keenly aware that my emotional reactions were anything but perfect. Mother and Father would be astonished and perplexed about my thoughts, my feelings, and my reactions! I had always been satisfied with my conduct, my feelings, and my choices, following my heart as I had been taught. Now it felt like my heart had betrayed me and was breaking. I didn't know what to do, and I felt completely betrayed and guilty for what I felt. Something was wrong. I was not, after all, perfect. I still had much to learn about how to evaluate what was going on in and around me.

I learned that perfection was having the courage to be present with my own pain and to examine my misguided or misunderstood beliefs to find the higher perspective. I had to once again unite my heart and mind together to find another way forward that was connected to my birthright of peace. And that required being willing to look at how I viewed myself and have the courage and the willpower to make changes within me that were causing so much distress. The distress and unhappiness were not held in the situation; they were held in my perspective of the situation. I found that changing my perspective made an enormous difference in my attitude and in how I actually began to feel.

Perfection is never found in being a certain way all the time; perfection is the process and practice of continually returning to the heart and the values of Love, especially when confronted with difficult or challenging situations that are there to help growth and evolution. Grandmother Mary frequently used the Pleiadian principle of seeing the highest version of me and using the power of sound through her words and tones to help me manifest the highest version of myself. She would comment on something positive I was doing or how well I had accomplished something or sometimes just hum a song out loud. I received the vibration and responded. Slowly I began to see how necessary my staying behind was, not only for the family, but for myself. I needed to use my gifts and talents to guide little Timaeus, supporting his path while following my own. And I needed to open my heart to receiving Timaeus' love and respect, which he actually did provide from the time he was very, very small.

We developed an unbreakable bond, both from being who we were and for supporting each other's understanding the true reality of our experience as Pleiadians living lives as humans on Earth. I had needed to make a radical change in perspective to remember who I was and begin again to live in the higher version of myself. This shift was necessary for me to regain my self-worth and live up to my potential. As I changed my thoughts, my guilt for reacting emotionally to my situation faded, and I recovered my sense of stability, slowly recognizing the opportunity before me and releasing my belief that I had been abandoned. This change of perspective was all that was needed to stop my heart and mind from acting separately and return me to a peaceful unity within myself. I stopped crying and began to sing again, which always brought me to a place of peace and contentment.

I want to share with you what I see about your world today. You have been taught to think before feeling. You have even been taught to ignore your feelings and that you are selfish if you pay attention to what you feel. But your feelings are your guidance. When you feel good feelings, you are in harmony with who you really are; when you feel bad feelings, you are being guided to change something within yourself. If you ignore what you feel, your mind will always lead you through loops and tangles of what you have experienced before or what you have been trained to think rather than opening itself to the heart's wisdom and guidance that is present. Your heart will always rebalance what is out of harmony, if you get your mind and your beliefs out of the way. One of your greatest gifts is the wisdom of the heart, which is connected to Source and will always guide you and keep you safe no matter what is happening all around you.

Try to remember what I shared with you about duality—everything that seems opposite and separate is just representing two sides of the same coin. Even the darkness is not opposite from the light; my parents always reminded me that darkness is only the absence of light. One side of the symbolic coin shows darkness, and one side of the coin shows light. You are all beings of light, but sometimes you can only see the side of the coin where light is missing and you must turn it over to find your light again. The symbolism of looking at both sides of a coin helps you to realize that it is one coin and that you are whole. You have the choice to align with the lighter side of yourself or to focus on the absence of light that you feel or perceive. The choice is always there to focus on the side of light!

Your heart and your mind are also two sides of the one

coin; each side has something to contribute to the whole, but you must honor and use them both together. You will find they work in perfect balance and harmony when you allow the heart to lead the way. That is the natural order for your evolution. Perfection can only be found in the living energy of the present moment, not in looking at some point in your perceived past or longing for an imagined future. The now moment provides perfection when you see clearly both sides of every coin. And when you follow your heart in each now moment, you are acting in perfection.

CHAPTER NINE

ENERGY & VIBRATION

Y LITTLE BROTHER, TIMAEUS, was drawn to the stars from the moment he was born. He would stare at them for hours, just watching the sparkle of the light as they twinkled in the night sky above him. He also responded to the energy of certain stars; some seemed to cause him distress, and some seemed to make him feel joyful. He would laugh as if being bathed in the energy of a particular star at times. I watched, fascinated at Timaeus' interaction with the stars. He was responding to their light at an energetic level. He seemed to truly know that he came from the stars and that they were part of him!

As Timaeus grew into a small boy, he was quiet and deep. It was obvious to me that he was always listening to and feeling everything around him, not only here on this planet, but he also listened to messages from the cosmos. He felt his way through life, moment-by-moment as the energies changed. Of course, we both had been taught the truth that everything is energy, and that time is a deceptive illusion, but Timaeus seemed to grasp that understanding at a deeper and more personal level even before he could speak. He was in tune with the energies of the universe, and he actually lived by following the energies.

Knowing that everything is energy and acting appropriately by paying attention to energy are two very different things. We are each made of energy. How I manifest myself and how you manifest yourself also has to do with our energetic makeup and how we make choices to use the gift of our own energies. But most people, not only in my time but also in your time today, ignore energy as if it does not exist. People tend to focus on what they perceive through their five physical senses—what they can see, hear, taste, smell, or touch. Very few people today are like Timaeus, who could feel the energy around him, as well as the new energy that was arriving. But you can, when you explore your own energetic makeup and notice how energies around you are always changing, always providing messages for how to proceed in your life.

Both Earth and the Universe bring in different energies to play with and guide your lives. I learned to associate color with certain vibrational frequencies, choosing the color that worked best for specific days or specific situations. While I dressed in plain clothes that were mostly neutral in color, as was the custom of my time, I put various colors of flowers in my hair and found other ways to use the vibration of different colors in my life. I knew that the blue vibration brings a sense of trust, which helped me to feel calm. I knew that the pink vibration carries the energy of Love. Yellow made me feel joyful. Red stirred me into movement and activity. Green is calming and I used that energy for rebalancing or inner healing. White made me pay attention to the truth in my heart and discern the difference between my beliefs and the illusions on Earth. Truth, which is profoundly simple, was always made clear in the energy of the color white. Purple has a strong energy of transformation, and I called on that energy whenever I found myself in an uncomfortable situation. With my own intention and purple energy, I could usually change my discomfort in any situation. But my favorite color was gold, which my Grandmother explained to me is the color of grace. As Grandmother Mary taught me, when one focuses on gold (or grace), everything begins to flow as it should. The colors used together help you find your way to personal balance and Love. You just have to trust (blue) that you and the truth of everything happening (white) will always be ok. This brings the energy of grace (gold), and when grace is present you find your way to live the Way of Love (pink). Mother used to always remind me, "Love is the answer to all of your questions or challenges, and we return to that state of Love through grace."

Everyone needs grace in their lives, for living on Earth is a challenge, especially if you remember the freedom of being other places in the universe. Sometimes it was hard for me to understand exactly what my purpose was or why I was here. My father had moved on; my mother had gone to France to teach. I was mostly content living with Grandmother Mary, and my time with her was very precious to me, although as explained, initially I struggled with being left behind. I understood my responsibility to help care for Timaeus and guide him to grow into a fine boy, but I knew there was something more. I longed to find it. I knew it was there, yet it took me a very long time to realize exactly where and what it was.

It was years before I had a real opportunity to search for my higher purpose. My dreams of going to the Magdalene School in Egypt had been replaced by my responsibility to help raise my little brother while my mother was teaching in other countries. And, of course, my being with Timaeus was a gift to me. He was a very special being, and I really enjoyed my duties in helping to guide him. As Grandmother Mary reminded me, I did not lose an opportunity in Egypt; I gained the opportunity of being with, helping to guide, and receiving Love from Timaeus.

As Timaeus became a young man, he was drawn to the astrological teaching and research schools in Egypt. He wanted nothing more than to go there and study the stars and how they affected people on Earth. As he had been a quiet child, it had been easy to keep Timaeus occupied and away from public scrutiny or interest. Now as he grew older and more interested in exploring esoteric teachings, he was more in danger from political adversaries, who still kept an eye on our family. If attention were drawn to him, they would believe he could potentially be a threat because of who his father had been. We suspected that he may have been watched, and therefore he kept mostly out of sight. It was I who usually went into the village if there was a need, while Timaeus stayed at home with our grandmother. On rare occasions, Grandmother Mary would go into the village on her own, and after one such visit, we discovered that she had made arrangements for Timaeus that would bring an important change into our lives.

It happened one day after one of her rare village trips. When she came home, Grandmother Mary announced that she had arranged for Timaeus to go to Alexandria and study the stars and the science of how they impact humanity. Grandmother Mary had connected with some of the other women who had studied with Mother's teachers at the Magdalene school before she married my father. They provided references for Timaeus and promised to have them delivered to the most gifted, wise, and heart-based teachers in Egypt, where Grandmother Mary planned to send her grandson. Plans were made and everything was arranged. Our uncle would take care of the transportation. They would depart at night, under cover of darkness so that their trip would not be impeded. Timaeus was excited, of course. This decision to study in Egypt eventually helped Timaeus to grow into his true purpose of showing humanity how energy affects everything and everyone and is always changing. He even authored a book about how connecting with Nature can help people achieve their soul purpose. My brother, Timaeus, was one of the few who, through his understanding of energy and connection, helped bring the idea of how the energy of place affects people's lives. It was an important contribution, but few today know that it was my Pleiadian brother who brought that wisdom to

Earth. His fascination with the stars guided him all of his life, and although I missed him when our paths separated, I understood that we were always connected in unity through Love. Timaeus' path was to go to Egypt to study the stars. Grandmother soon announced to me that my path was to join my mother in France. I was content.

Pleiadians have always tried to help humanity understand the concepts I am explaining here: that everything is energy and that all energies have intelligence and vibration. Before my time, Pleiadians shared this wisdom with many people across the planet, including the Mayan people in Central America, the Dogon in Africa, and the Cherokee in North America. It seems people who are more closely connected to Nature find it easier to understand the concept of changing energies because they witness that in Nature on a daily basis. They learn to work with every energy that arrives in a way that is harmonious rather than trying to control it to meet their own desires. This is an enormous problem today. Because of the Christian myth and the myths of other religions and fundamentalists groups, most people believe that they have the right to control animals, plants, and Nature in general. They do not realize that they are part of Nature and that they, too, are made of specific energies and must take responsibility to choose how to respond to energies that arrive from the stars or how to move to a specific place that is more harmonious with their own energies. Most people across the planet are ignorant of this important truth, even though Pleiadians have been sharing this wisdom with humanity for thousands of years.

Here on this planet of choice, people are able to decide whether they will interact with higher or lower vibrations every moment of every day, including the energy of other people and place (my brother's discovery). Of course, the cosmic goal is always to choose the higher vibration in order to obtain an elevated consciousness, but I find most people are too lazy or in too much of a hurry to slow down enough to actually feel the energies that are always present. Humans are not very good at seeing and understanding the symbols that manifest to guide you even though they are all around you. The universe always provides symbolic clues in many ways to let you know which energies are presenting themselves for your benefit.

What I want to share with those who are reading my words is that understanding energy is a gift to yourself! When you understand your own energy and work to discover the various vibrations of other different energies, it empowers you to make clearer and better choices in every moment of your life. You choose better places to live; you choose work that is aligned with your heart; you choose relationships that are more harmonious. You also have a chance to act from the higher or lower vibration of your own energy, so it is advantageous to study and understand the energy that you carry here in this life, with both its high and low possibilities, and how your energy interacts with and affects all other energies.

Following the description of the importance of water, light, movement, and sound, the study of energy and vibration makes more sense. Each of the above elements displays a particular energetic quality and how its vibration can change. When you begin to work with the energy of who you are and the energy that is presented to you daily in life, you gain an appreciation of the power you carry as a divine spark of light and how to use that power for Love and the cosmic goal of your conscious evolution. Everything is energy, and energy is everything!

CHAPTER TEN

SOUL & SPIRIT

WHEN I WAS A YOUNG WOMAN and Timaeus was firmly established in Egypt with his star studies, Grandmother Mary and I made our way to France to join Mother. I was glad we were going and had no reservations about leaving what had always been my home. I knew that Earth was my home for now and that at some point, I would return to the stars from where I came. It was exciting to be going somewhere completely different here on Earth, and traveling over water as well!

The journey over the sea was somewhat arduous because of the season in which we departed. The timing presented itself, and we knew that we needed to go. I do not need to say more about that; I am sure you understand that political pressures can encourage and hasten such decisions, even when one has been waiting for the right moment and the heart finally speaks. My uncle provided both the transportation and his company to help us get settled into a new life, and we were grateful. Being on the ocean was also delightful to me in spite of the frequent storms and turbulence, for I always connect with water. I loved watching the sparkles of light play off the water as I gazed out to the sea. I also felt the seeds of freedom growing in me in the same way one can feel movement in stillness. I was about to step onto a land that I intuitively knew would resonate with my own energy more than my homeland had done. I was about to establish my new life in a land that would keep me safe and allow me to grow at the same time. And after years of feeling someone was missing in my daily routine, I was about to reunite with my beloved mother.

The reunion was beautiful! Grandmother and my uncle stood back to allow me the experience of reconnection with just the two of us—Mother and me— for a short while as we both remembered the link between our souls and the journey of our spirits. We were once again physically together!

I feel I need to provide some clarity here about soul and spirit because there seems to be a lot of confusion around understanding those two terms in your modern world. The spirit is your direct connection to Source and the energy that guides your path; this is why your life is often called a spiritual journey. Your spirit could also be called the highest version of yourself. It is like a whisper in the wind, or the gentle breeze that brushes your cheek, encouraging you to look or listen in a certain direction. The spirit is light, and bright, and ever moving. It can be seen as the potential movement in stillness before the actual movement begins. People say their spirit is "broken" when they lose the courage or willpower to move forward in continued growth. Of course, your spirit can never be broken; you simply feel disconnected from it because you feel disconnected from Source. Your spirit guides you when you listen to and reconnect with your heart, where all wisdom lives. Your heart joins you to Source.

The soul is your essence, the part of you that experiences all lifetimes in all dimensions and is whole. The soul is who you truly are; it is the beginning and the end, the alpha and the omega, the part of you that can never, ever be destroyed. It is through your soul that you integrate all of your life experiences, or the parallel lives you have in multiple dimensions. The soul is multidimensional. It can be anywhere and everywhere at once. It is the part of you that remembers what it is like to be free, to fly, to think about a place and instantly be there. The soul has no boundaries of time or space. It is the part of you that actually experiences the true reality without the distractions of various life experiences in your current life or in multiple other dimensions, although it is absolutely present in all of your dimensional life experiences. Because the soul is the part that helps you to integrate all of yourself, it is important to understand exactly what the soul is and what it does. The soul holds all aspects of who you are and helps you to integrate them to feel complete. Integration means joining all the parts of yourself from all dimensions together as you remember who you truly are in the larger reality. This is the soul's job.

In my time on Earth and even now in your modern world, integration of all parallel lives does not usually happen until a person dies. The power of belief on Earth can block the ability to accept the larger picture of multidimensional reality. People are often afraid of losing who they consider themselves to be in this life by integrating other aspects of themselves existing in other dimensions. It can be confusing until you remember that you are divine sparks of light, and every aspect of you in every dimension truly reflects who you are, not just who you believe yourself to be here in the third dimension. Each experience contributes to your learning and growth. Accepting multidimensional experiences and integrating them into yourself is part of your cosmic goal and leads you to the path of Ascension through merging your physical form and your light body. Clinging to the belief that your perceived third dimensional identity is all of who you are contributes to Ascending through the process of death, rather than Ascending as my family did by understanding how to merge all aspects of yourself multidimensionally.

Most people are also full of lower vibratory attachment to feelings they have not processed or transcended because of their beliefs—feelings like guilt and jealousy and anger and frustration and grief. These feelings are meant to guide everyone to change their perspectives and open their hearts, but most people ignore the messages of these feelings, either blaming someone else for how they feel or distracting themselves from the inner work that is being offered through uncomfortable feelings. They are afraid of feeling something different even if it could be better, although they long for it. This is one reason why Mother so often said, "Fear not!" She knew (and knows today) that fear is the opposite of Love and the greatest blocker of conscious evolution. Letting go of or working through your fear is the gateway to achieving all that you are as a being of light and Love.

Today there are portals of energetic opportunity opening to humanity to provide (and provoke) evolutionary choices. You have achieved enough awareness to let go of who you think you are. You have achieved enough courage to face the parts of yourself that still contain lower vibrations and change them. You may even be somewhat driven to recognize and examine other aspects of yourself existing in other dimensions to clear old traumas or claim gifts that you can use in your current experience. As you begin to truly understand the principles of multidimensionality, how it works, and that you exist in many dimensions at once, you can begin to integrate them and free yourself from attachment to the third dimensional experience of being only a human on Earth. You open your heart to remembering who you are as a divine spark of light and an emerging cosmic citizen! You can recognize that your soul is calling all parts of you to integrate so that you can come Home through the process of Ascension in the way my father did, rather than waiting on death to bring a clearer vision. I will speak more about Ascension later. For now, I want to finish my story about my reunion with my mother, Mary Magdalene.

To achieve her life purpose on Earth of continuing the

teachings about Love that she and my father had come here to share, Mother knew that I could not live with her. She knew there was still danger even in places in France for those who shared higher wisdom that was not accepted by societies of the time. Much of her life was spent in seclusion in Nature, allowing those who were energetically aligned with the truth to approach and learn. Sometimes, like my father, she would travel to various regions that were energetically aligned with the truth and through her simple presence, open people's hearts to the true reality. There were special regions in France where that was possible and portals where the energy encouraged others to come together in unity rather than living in fear with that overriding sense of separation that is so prevalent on Earth.

After our initial reunion, Mother greeted her beloved mother-in-law, my Grandmother Mary, and they embraced. She greeted and thanked my uncle for our safe passage. She then guided all of us into the safety of her home to rest, nourish ourselves, and share together. Of course, she wanted to know about Timaeus, even though they were energetically connected. She wanted to hear the stories of our experiences with him, and she wanted to know about my life as well. As the day drew to a close, my uncle departed, ready to leave this gathering of such powerful divine feminine energy and continue his journey on his own path of trade and exploration. Grandmother Mary and I thanked him for our safe transport and his Love and support.

We rested, ate, and shared for many days before Mother announced that it was time to visit a special place. Traveling westward, we followed the energetic lines of Earth until we reached one of Mother's favorite communities, which was full of people who were also sharing father's and her teachings. She encouraged me to find my own connections with people there, trusting that I could and would find the energy that resonated most with me. I discovered a particularly wonderful connection with an older couple, and it was soon agreed that I would live with them, at least at first, seeing and learning from Mother when she visited. Grandmother felt called to another village close by where she resonated with the energy of the land and people, and she settled there. Grandmother Mary and I still saw each other frequently and sat together, as it was only a short walk between the villages where each of us settled. For the rest of Grandmother Mary's life, we were never physically apart for long, and we were always energetically connected. I always knew when she was thinking of me or silently calling to me to come and visit. Her messages arrived in my heart and stirred me into action, so I would quickly walk the short distance to be with her. Grandmother Mary always was and continued to be my guiding light on this planet and in the universe, and she has been Pia's guiding light throughout her life also because of our connection. As Pia integrated me, Grandmother Mary reached out to guide her in Love, too.

You could say that our spiritual journey took us away from home and what was familiar, and that would be true. However, it was in what was unfamiliar that we grew as we gained a deeper sense of community, unity, and unconditional Love among people whom we trusted and who protected us from those who might be frightened of what we represented. Outwardly, we were like anyone else. But you and I both know that we radiated light that was much brighter than most others of the time, and that light had to be honored and protected until it was time for our souls to completely integrate and call us Home. Most of you who are called to read this book also radiate light that is brighter than others around you, and like me, you are here to be of service. Meanwhile, I had more life to live, more service to offer, and more lessons to learn.

Part of my journey towards the unfamiliar, the pathway led by my spirit to listen to my heart, guided me to an even deeper integration of myself through connection to another–a specific other–who offered me explorations of physical expressions of Love as well as the unconditional Love I shared with everyone. I did not meet him immediately, for my spirit led me first to increase my awareness of resonance and non-resonance with both people and place. Although I was past the age most women of my time married and had children, it was necessary for me to explore resonance by being with people whose frequency supported my own in a place that I felt was beautiful and protective. I found that in France, in the little village where I now lived as a young woman and where I met my soon-to-be husband. And with every visit from my mother, I was learning more about the soul's journey, the process of integration, and the nature of Love.

The land around me was more vibrant and alive in my new village than the land where I had been born and grew into a woman. There were more trees here than in my homeland, and I talked to them every day as I walked ancient pathways in rolling hills. Flowers exploded with colors so sparkling and bright they dazzled my eyes. I touched and thanked them for sharing their beauty with me. Even the water in streams I passed seemed to speak to me, and I often sat by a favorite river listening to the secrets the river had to share. I knew that my human body was mostly water, so connecting with the river's water seemed as though I was recognizing another part of myself. I do know that all energy is connected, and I know that water on this planet carries messages from one place to another. I shared my Love with the river as it shared its secrets with me.

As I spent more time in Nature, I discovered more about who I truly was. I discovered the answer to my childhood guess about my own scent. I am indeed connected to the lilies that I was drawn to visit in my childhood walks with my father and on my walks every day as a young woman in France. I loved their beauty, their subtle sweet smell, and I always felt they had something to teach me.

As my stay lengthened and my new village became home for me, I felt the safe embrace of my community and the inner calling to be more open for deeper experiences with the man who supported and harmonized with my energy. For me to join with another, the resonance had to match on all levels—spiritually first, of course, and then at the mental and feeling levels, and finally the possible resonance of our physical bodies together. My mother and father radiated that kind of resonance and always demonstrated that Love is the most beautiful and powerful force in the universe.

Nevertheless, I was somewhat surprised when such a divine and lasting gift offering me that kind of Love arrived in my own life! He and I were able to join ourselves with such deep resonance, connection, and remembrance that together we integrated much of our parallel selves in other dimensions. In fact, we integrated so well as a couple that we managed to live and grow together until we Ascended in the way Father, Mother, and Grandmother Mary did, leaving behind our two children, with whom we had shared all the Pleiadian principles for living. Our souls were united, and we went Home together.

When you think about your own spirit and your own soul, try to remember that you are on a journey of exploration of Love. Following Love will support your remembering and fully becoming who you really are! Nothing else really matters as deeply as this fundamental understanding of life. And remember my mother's teaching,

> *"Everything is energy, and your energy affects everyone and everything on the planet, so be loving in all that you think and do. Be conscious of how you live, as you have an energetic effect of others in every moment. Always live from a place of non-judgment and unconditional Love."*

CHAPTER ELEVEN

INTEGRATION

I DID NOT FULLY UNDERSTAND the process of integration until I moved to France and was able to have deep conversations about the process with my mother. I knew that integration involved the power of Love, but I did not realize that the most important element of the integrative process is loving oneself. Once I changed my perspective and recovered from my twelve-year-old self-induced emotional feelings of abandonment when my mother left our homeland to continue her work, I had no problem loving myself. I liked who I was, and I liked even more who I was becoming as I learned and evolved. By the time I was a young woman, I had a very good sense of what today you call self-esteem that stayed with me all of my life and helped me be clear about choosing my energetic partner in life in France.

But I see today that people have lost not only their

remembrance that they are divine sparks of light, but also their sense of simply being loved and accepted as they are. Everywhere I look I see people struggling to hide something about themselves that they view as inappropriate or not acceptable. Some are concerned that they are not beautiful. Some are concerned that they are too poor. Some are concerned because they feel they are not able to do what they know they should do or because they are doing something they know in their hearts that they should not be doing. Most are worried because they feel they are not lovable. The reason for this is because they have disconnected from Source and do not recognize that they are always loved and supported by the universe. All they have to do is have the courage to use their emotions to change what is out of balance within themselves, which usually arises because of erroneous belief systems. Modern people, like people of my day, are afraid to look too deeply into themselves and discover things they do not like or accept about themselves, or they are afraid others will not love them if others see the things they are working to transcend. Most people do not yet understand that their emotions are actually signals to change something inside of them—a perspective, a belief, or a reaction. I spoke about this earlier, but I will say more now to help you understand. Emotions are those feelings that make you uncomfortable or unhappy. Emotions are simply what you would call "sign posts" today to help you realize that you have more work to accomplish on your personal journey of evolution and growth. They are there to point out what is out of balance so that you can return to calm and peaceful feelings within you and then radiate that peace into the world through choices that come from unconditional Love– for yourself and for others. Working with what you feel in each now moment helps you to acknowledge, listen to, and act upon what your emotions are telling you. And achieving this, changes your beliefs about yourself and the world.

People are usually trained by others and society to believe that they are not perfect or whole the way they are, which leads to judging both yourself and others, creating even more separation. It is the belief systems that everyone relies upon to define your reality that prevent a smooth integration of all aspects of yourself. Lack of integration skills also comes from an attachment to who you believe yourself to be here in the third dimension, another belief system that is limiting you on Earth. You are so much more than your physical form, your mind and thoughts, your emotional makeup, or even your spiritual values. You exist in multiple dimensions simultaneously, and evolving into a cosmic citizen requires an awareness of and integration of the aspects of yourself that are simultaneously happening in other dimensions while you are fully engaged simultaneously in your life here on Earth.

Integration means to take various parts that you imagine are separate and blend them harmoniously into the whole. You must open your hearts and your minds to accept that there is more to you than what you believe or what you experience only here in the third dimension. One way to do this is through what my mother, Mary Magdalene, so frequently taught,

"Accept everything simply as an experience without judging it, but do your part to participate in the moment through conscious choices of response that are for the highest good for all."

You can always choose to see things simply as experiences rather than viewing them as challenges, but even challenges should be seen as potential gifts that are opportunities for growth. This is the pathway to evolution, and this will start your integration process. As my mother always shared, "There is no past or future, and it is being present in the now that allows all healing to take place."

When you first begin to have awareness of other aspects of yourself, you may be surprised or feel disoriented. Awareness may come as short reflections that you see but may not be able to explain or as insights that are deeply meaningful to you. Do not try to analyze them; simply accept them as revelations that arrive to support your integration, and trust that you are inviting all aspects of yourself to integrate so that you can become the multidimensional being you are designed to be. Once this process begins in earnest, you will find that more and more revelations and insights will come to you, and you will feel more comfortable in expanding your description of who you believe yourself to be!

Most of the work of integration is very personal and individual. But on occasion, when you are well matched in resonance and Love with another person, aspects that are being shared with each other in other dimensions will reveal themselves to you in this one in a way that both people know and understand what those aspects mean and how they bring both gifts and challenges to overcome. The strength of a heart-joined relationship can open portals of understanding where recognition pours through and is validated through mutual sharing. Integrative experiences do not need to be validated, but sometimes it is comforting to find that someone close to you also remembers and shares the recognition of larger, more expansive aspects of your experiences. This can also bring both people closer together through sharing your increased understanding and acceptance of each other and of the greater reality that is showing itself to you.

Whether recognized individually or recognized together with a beloved person, each experience that comes leads you closer to realization of the truth. And as my father said, "You shall know the truth, and the truth will set you free." You cannot hide from it because it is part of who you are. When you move closer to the truth (because you are part of the truth) there is nothing to fear; there is only Love and more Love, and every experience carries you closer to that feeling of freedom and peace that is always present with true unconditional Love.

Integrating myself and what I know through Pia's eyes has been interesting. While I am living an experience in what you would perceive as ancient times in France, Pia is having a modern-day experience on an island in the Mediterranean. She is living on an island that claims to be the birth place of an ancient goddess of Love called Venus. We are having different experiences, but they are happening simultaneously, and we are both aware of our shared and differing perspectives. Today, as I dictate this message through Pia's hands into this book, is a day when Pia read many dire predictions for things falling apart in the time in which she is living. Because of her aware integration with me, she immediately incorporated my mother, Mary Magdalene's teaching that everything is just an experience that leads you closer to realization of the truth. Pia responded to what she read with feelings of excitement about coming changes rather than reacting with any type of fear. This is exactly what my mother and father tried to help humanity understand. Fear not! Everything is for your good, but you have to do your part to participate with the energies through conscious, aware responses and choices.

Pia has the quotes my father and mother gave her years ago now framed on her desk. I see and feel her looking at those quotes as if they are living messages from her parents, and I know that she has fully integrated my life as Sarah as part of who she is. She has deepened her understanding about the messages Mother and Father gave her, which are repeated again and again throughout this book because of their value and importance,

> *"The truth will set you free, but first it will test you to the limit. The secret to this test is to love it all."*

CHAPTER TWELVE

WHO ARE YOU?

WHO ARE YOU? I have told you that I am Sarah, daughter of Mary Magdalene and Jesus of Nazareth, but I am also so much more. You are, too.

I am also part of Pia, as she is part of me and many other multiple aspects of energy. You, also, are more than who you see yourself to be in the third dimension. You are not just a mother, father, daughter, son, sister, brother, worker, employer, volunteer, or member of a certain church or group. You are not defined by your choice of religion, color of your skin, the country in which you live, who you choose to vote for, or the other choices you make every day according to your beliefs at the moment. You are not any one thing; you are all of those things, as well as the aspects of yourself you are integrating from other dimensional experiences. You are much larger, more vast, and multi-faceted than you have imagined yourselves to be through your third dimensional eyes!

In your present Earthly experience, your physical body is mostly water, but you also carry fire, or light, from the stars. This is why you are a divine spark of light, but you must learn how to properly use the water of your being to communicate and connect with others. It is through honoring the water of who you are and how you share your gifts that your light shines more brightly. Fire and water may seem opposites to you, but remember that all opposites can exist together harmoniously in unity. This is just another example of how you can use duality for your benefit and service to others. Honor the water you are and the water of others. Shine your light and share the brightness of your highest self with the world. You must choose wisely what you put into your own water so that you do not pollute it with things that do not support communication, flow, balance, and health. You must learn that how you share your water through the tones and the words you choose affects others, because your tones ripple out into the water of others, impacting them both here on Earth and in other dimensions as well. Remember that sound manifests reality so you want to be really careful with the sounds you share with others. This entire Earth journey for your soul is an experience of learning and integrating these concepts and other things that you are learning. Your experience on Earth is a journey of service, yet it is also a very large mission for your personal evolution and learning about how you, as energy, affect all other energies here and throughout the cosmos!

Have you discovered your scent and how your essence radiates into the world? Have you discovered your way of returning to the heart after experiencing emotional guidance and necessary change? Have you discovered how you give Love and how you receive Love in your relationships? Have you discovered your favorite color or favorite smell, or the energies that call you to be who you are? My father primarily used the energy of the colors of purple for transformation and green for healing when he was here on Earth. My mother preferred using the pink energy of Love and the red energy of movement. Grandmother Mary worked with and radiated the blue energy of trust. And as I told you earlier, I had an affinity with the golden color of grace. Pia has chosen the yellow energy of joy as her primary energy to explore and expand on her Earth journey. What is the color and energy that you are here to work with and explore? They are all available to you, and you can utilize their energies in different now moments, as your soul calls you and your spirit directs you! These are important things to learn about yourself, for everything you can know about your own energy helps you to utilize it better in service to self and others.

Each of you is experiencing a life as someone else simultaneously along with your current third dimensional experience; in fact, in the larger reality where time does not exist you are experiencing multiple other lives in multiple dimensions. As developing humans who are becoming conscious of multidimensionality at an increasing rate of awareness and understanding, you are incorporating all of the aspects of yourself through your process of integration in order to return to the wholeness that will arise from your awareness and your work in this current experience.

When I walked the Earth, I only thought of myself as Sarah, daughter, granddaughter, and sister until I moved to France. It was there in the resonance that land held for me and my personal energy that I became deeply immersed in discovering and connecting with other aspects of who I was, recognizing them through little glimpses, and then, as living visions. It was my divine connection with my husband that enlarged and deepened that experience for both of us. It was also there that I learned how to truly relate through Love with all aspects of myself and with another. I want to share that possibility with you as you begin to see and understand how tremendous multidimensional reality truly is and how powerful you are in navigating it when you make higher vibrational choices!

Your power is connected to your alignment with Love. Without unconditional Love, your essence is trapped in a world that is controlled by your beliefs and your fears. This is why my mother, Mary Magdalene, encouraged people then and encourages people today to simply love all experiences, accepting that they are for your education and evolution. Accepting everything as it is produces more fullness in your lives and helps you to be more receptive to what presents itself for your growth. It is also for this reason that my mother continually counselled everyone to listen to their hearts because they are directly connected to Source. She continues offering that guidance through Pia and others today. The truth is that your heart contains great wisdom that guides you to live a heart-centered life.

It can be unsettling to suddenly discover another part of yourself, but it can also be joyful! Remember that you are on an evolutionary journey, and do your best to be open to what the universe brings you. Multidimensionality is an enormous reality, and it certainly cannot be contained in a set of parameters of limited thinking, explanations, or beliefs. By definition, multidimensionality is what Pia calls in modern terms "being outside of the box!" I use Pia's words here to clarify my point.

Freedom awaits you on your journey to other dimensions throughout the universe. Be free my friends! As you remember the wholeness of who you are and reclaim your power through being and giving unconditional Love, you will find your freedom through exercising clear, positive choices and refusing to be limited. Remember that limitations are part of the third dimensional illusion, and you are working to free yourself from the limited third dimensional reality. Returning to awareness and experiencing the larger true multidimensional reality is the way to complete your cosmic goal. Everything is available for you to experience and support your growth into becoming your true self.

Because there is no such thing as time and the concept of time is part of the illusion that keeps you trapped in your box of beliefs, you may understand when I say that Now is the moment to release your attachment to any limited versions of yourself! Open your heart and your mind to all of your experiences, as they will lead you to discover your connection to other aspects of yourself. There are no good or bad experiences, although you certainly experience the polarity of pain or pleasure with each one. But there is learning in both the pain and in the pleasure of your third dimensional experiences, as long as you neither avoid nor attach to what is happening. Be present. Be open. Be aware. And use the power of your Love to transcend what does not resonate with the truth of who you are as a divine spark of light, connected to each other and to Source. Ultimately, as you discover and remember who you are and the gifts you carry, you will find that you are simply and purely, Love. Be that Love and let your light shine into the world! It will set you free.

CHAPTER THIRTEEN

GOING HOME: ASCENSION

FOR A LONG TIME, modern Christians have talked about Ascension as though my father was the only one who ever achieved it. You even believe that my father was a god who could do things that you cannot do, but this is simply not true, for you are divine also. Many people other than my father have understood the process of raising their vibration and integrating all aspects of themselves, thereby Ascending into what we Pleiadians call a Rainbow body form. A Rainbow body form is one that incorporates all the energetic colors of all your experiences multidimensionally. It is a combination of a lighter physical body with your etheric light body. My father came here to demonstrate to you what you are capable of and show you how to achieve Ascending with your body into a lighter form that can be anywhere and can achieve everything you wish. My

Grandmother Mary, my mother, my brother Timaeus, and I myself (along with my beloved husband) also Ascended in this manner. The people of my region and time simply accepted that path of energetic change as both real and possible because we demonstrated it to them over our time together. The only written mention of any of my family's Ascension experiences (other than my father's Ascension) comes from notations by scholars in Egypt who mentioned briefly in their academic works that my brother Timaeus simply "disappeared," leaving questions and mystery about who he was.

Although there is no written record of our Ascension into a Rainbow body, there are many stories in your Earthly cultures of others besides my father and our family who attained the ability to Ascend into a Rainbow body. Those who achieved this state and Ascended with their bodies have always been seen by others on your planet as sages, special people, or teachers whom you believe achieved a miracle or the impossible. But Ascending with your body is neither impossible nor a miracle; it is simply a matter of making your vibration so high that your body changes into a lighter form, as I have explained. It is a natural process you are entitled to experience as a divine spark of light! When you achieve this, you will be able to travel anywhere in the universe or be multiple places at once. You will be capable of shapeshifting as you manifest into whatever form the energy of the now moment requires. You will have simply become energetic wave forms of Love!

The Ascension process happens when you turn the

focus of your attention to your energetic body and away from your experiences of pleasure or pain, whether that pain is physical or emotions or thoughts that need attention and correction. Focus upon integrating all aspects of who you are without assigning "good" or "bad" meanings to them. I have told you that my father chose to experience the worst physical pain to show others how to transcend it, while my mother demonstrated to those most closely associated with her how to transcend extreme emotional pain. Yet the people of the time could only relate to my father's Ascension as death when he went through the transformation process except for the few who understood his teachings when he appeared again in a lighter form; my mother was mostly ignored or dismissed during this time. No one believed that it was possible for my father to walk the Earth again, so to them, it was a miracle that they could never achieve themselves. Many did not believe it was true even when they saw it because their belief systems confused them and they were unable to explain what they witnessed.

And so, stories have been passed down through religions that my father was a god and thereby able to Ascend with his body, but that he alone could do this. Your religions have been misinforming people even about the purpose of my father's actions. Your religions teach that my father "died for your sins." In a way that is true, if you understand that a sin is simply a mistake. It was a mistake for the authorities to try to kill my father, who was only here to bring more light and Love into the world. But that does not mean that his death is related to your "sins" or your mistakes. That is just a way of religions trying to make you feel guilty and more disconnected so that you can more easily be controlled. Your mistakes, as I have already said, are the way you learn and grow. They do not keep you from connecting to Source, or God. When you learn from something you have done incorrectly, you actually connect more deeply to Source. I would like to say that your religions do not understand that, but maybe they do. Maybe they know how the process works and just do not want you to understand or achieve it, for to be more connected directly to Source lessens their control over you and brings you more into unity. Such wisdom raises your consciousness, which is the cosmic goal. You have the right to know and understand the truth and to use it properly to assist in your own evolution and Ascension process!

Even your beliefs about the timing of Ascension, including my father's Ascension, are incorrect. Anyone can achieve Ascension with their body at any time, once you disengage from your attachment to the meaning of the duality of pleasure and pain and integrate all aspects of yourself through unconditional Love and acceptance, as I have explained. My father knew and understood that he would endure and transcend physical pain to teach others how to do this in the timing he choose for his own Ascension. Today everyone believes (because you have all been taught to believe this) that my father Ascended in what is celebrated as your Easter, in the Spring of the year near Equinox. But that is not true. The time of my father's Ascension was altered in your history to match ancient pagan spring rituals, turning them into more modern religious ceremonies. My father actually Ascended early in the winter month you call November, when the star system, the Pleiades, was closest to Earth. That was the energetic portal he chose and passed through on his Ascension journey. As you can see, your history and the dates you have been told are true, are not aligned with the true reality of events.

After our time on Earth in France, men in Rome altered the historical record of my father's Ascension, along with his actual physical arrival on Earth. Even before this, my mother frequently commented that humans need to see the larger picture, not just look at simple Earthly cycles or rituals. Humanity needs to recognize cosmic cycles and when the stars are aligned with Earth for the opening of consciousness and heart. Ascension with the body is more possible during these special periods of energetic alignment with Earth. My brother Timaeus was of the same opinion, having spent most of his life studying the stars. There are portals of opportunity when cosmic forces support expansion of consciousness, but it is always an individual choice whether to take those opportunities or to stay stuck in your belief systems about what is perceived as acceptable consensual reality. History is always rewritten for the benefit of those who wish to control humanity.

I will remind you that integration means joining all the parts of yourself together as you remember who you truly are. I am Sarah, Pleiadian daughter of Mary Magdalene and Jesus of Nazareth. But I also have other names related to my

Venusian experience, my Lemurian experience, my angelic experience, and of course, my parallel life as Pia. I share this with you because transparency is important when you want to live in truth and Love. I have not told you about my experience as a Lemurian or my experience on Earth's twin planet, Venus, nor my angelic experiences. Although those aspects are part of who I am, they are not relevant to this story. This story is about sharing what I have told you from the perspective of integrating myself as daughter of Mary Magdalene, daughter of Jesus of Nazareth, and Granddaughter of Mother Mary with Pia. There are other aspects of myself I have not shared as well. I am also part of an Interstellar Council, where I use an even different name that represents all points of difference merging into unity, which you perceive visually as the end point of your letter V. In that experience, I use a stronger voice. Listen to the song of my words and take them into your vibration. The truth will set you free.

The boundaries of who I am as Sarah, daughter of Mary Magdalene and Granddaughter of Mother Mary, were blurred in this life experience as Pia until she integrated and remembered that we are part of each other in the whole of reality. The blurring of lives stopped as I have filled Pia with all of my energy, my perspectives, and my story, and she has integrated other lifetimes as well, recognizing now that Mary Magdalene is her true mother as well as mine.

When I speak about Ascension and the integration that is required to Ascend into a Rainbow body form, I encourage you to release your concepts about time. A paradigm shift is needed for you to realize that time does not exist, and you did not exist as "someone else" in a previous life. All experiences are simultaneous, which is why I refer to your other experiences as parallel lives and why I share the story of my integration with Pia. They are happening in other dimensions at the same moment you are having your third dimensional experience as who you think you are. But it is this position of experiencing life on Earth that provides the opportunity for integrating all aspects of yourself and raising your vibration through making higher and higher choices in each moment. And it is this process that leads you, through the power of unconditional Love, to Ascend with your lighter body into a consciously evolved human with a Rainbow body and to attain cosmic citizenship and the freedom to move about the universe as you choose. Remember that you always have a choice to either hold on to your belief systems and remain in fear or to choose multidimensional truth and cosmic freedom. I remind you that part of your path to achieving Ascension and cosmic citizenship is to learn to flow through circumstances rather than resisting them. As my mother always shared, "This is the way to peace, as well as freedom."

Understanding how parallel realities *really* work supports blending your gifts and healing your challenges through unconditional Love and acceptance, as Grandmother Mary taught me to do and as Pia is doing now. This is the Way of Love, which brings a great sense of peace and calm, just as my mother, Mary Magdalene, always demonstrated. And in this current life experience as Pia who has integrated

Sarah, I/we are living from a place that is not based on expectations created from the past but on curiosity about possibilities for what can come next! As my parents Mary Magdalene and Jesus of Nazareth taught me long ago, with my integration as Sarah into Pia, she is learning to Love it all, even the hard parts. There is joy in that! And there is freedom.

My gift to you is my story and the reminder to Love it all. When you become unconditional Love, you Ascend to your highest form. I will end my story with repeating the most important teaching, which was repeated throughout this book, from my parents about the Way of Love:

"You shall know the Truth, and the Truth shall set you free....but first, it will test you to the ultimate"

— *Jesus of Nazareth*

"The secret of this test is to Love it all...for when you Love all, everything comes to you, and fear will disappear. Fear Not!"

— *Mary Magdalene*

ACKNOWLEDGMENTS

MY HEART IS FULL OF THANKS for my beloved Cullen, who has been with me not only on this life journey but also in many parallel lives. Thank you for your constant, unconditional Love expressed in so many ways, your support in my writing this and other books, and for your brilliant editing, which always provides a polished touch to the words telling the story. You are one of a kind here on Earth–both Pleiadian and human.

Thanks to my wonderful friend and magnificent graphic artist, Chris Molé of Book Savvy Studio for her perfect layout and graphic designs of cover and text. I am honored to have you on this journey with me, Chris.

I wish to thank my long-time amazing friend, Rebecca Gretz, for her ever-present support in all ways.

Last, but certainly not least, my profound gratitude to my other-world family:

Mother Mary (known by Sarah as Grandmother Mary) for appearing to me and speaking through me, with her call to speak the truth to all; Mary Magdalene, my true mother, for her guidance, wisdom, and dedication to justice and Love, who also speaks through me; to the Christ light whose unconditional Love has always over-lighted my spiritual path; to Sarah herself, who so beautifully tells her story in this book, and to their colleagues, the Pleiadian group, Laarkmaa, who work with Cullen and me today to help humanity evolve. I am grateful for your presence and Love in my life!

ABOUT THE AUTHOR

P IA ORLEANE, PH.D. is a former practicing Psychologist, Alternative Health Consultant, Pleiadian-Earth Energy Astrologer, Respected Intuitive, and award-winning author. Pia has the distinction of having won either a Nautilus "Better Books for a Better World" or a Coalition for Visionary Resources Gold award for every book she has ever published, as well as winning Gold awards for the Calendar and Card deck she and her husband, Cullen Baird Smith co-created. Together with Cullen Baird Smith, Pia co-authored the *Wisdom From the Stars Trilogy,* the divination book *Pleiadian-Earth Energy Astrology– Charting the Spirals of Consciousness,* the yearly *Pleiadian-Earth Energy Calendar,* and *The Original Pleiadian Wisdom Oracle Cards.* Pia also won the Coalition for Visionary Fiction Gold award for her book *Exit Plan and other Short Stories* and the Nautilus

Gold Award for *Sacred Retreat–Using Natural Cycles to Recharge Your Life,* now a classic on cycles of human life and divine feminine principles.

Pia and her husband, Cullen, live in Europe and work with the Pleiadian group, Laarkmaa, to bring higher awareness and evolutionary support everywhere in the world. You can find more about Pia's work and services here:

https://www.piaorleane.com

You can find more about Pia and Cullen's joint work with Laarkmaa and their services here:

https://www.laarkmaa.com

OTHER SOURCES
OF WISDOM

Nautilus "Better Books for a Better World" Gold Award-winning Classic

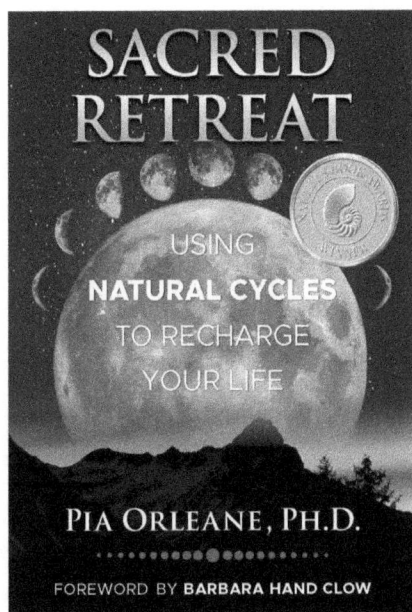

SACRED RETREAT
Using Natural Cycles to Recharge Your Life
by Pia Orleane, Ph.D.
Inner Traditions/Bear & Company, 2017
Rochester, VT
ISBN 978-1-59143-791-8

Coalition for Visionary Resources
Gold Award-winner
for Visionary Fiction

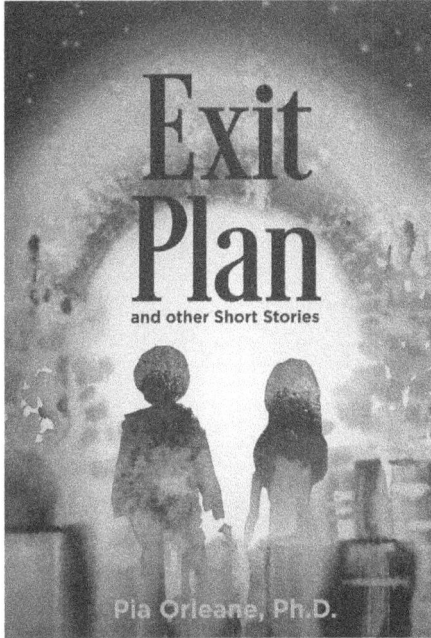

EXIT PLAN
and other Short Stories

by Pia Orleane, Ph.D.
Onewater Press, 2021
Santa Fe, NM;
ISBN 978-1-7367-35-8-8

WISDOM FROM THE STARS TRILOGY

Coalition for Visionary Resources
Gold Award-winning trilogy
by Pia Orleane, Ph.D. &
Cullen Baird Smith, including:

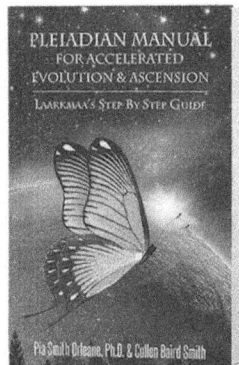

CONVERSATIONS WITH LAARKMAA
A Pleiadian View of the New Reality
Onewater Press, 2010, Santa Fe, NM
ISBN 978-0-9967835-0-7

REMEMBERING WHO WE ARE
Laarkmaa's Guidance on Healing the Human Condition
Onewater Press, 2015, Santa Fe, NM
ISBN 978-0-9967835-1-4

PLEIADIAN MANUAL FOR ACCELERATED EVOLUTION & ASCENSION
Onewater Press, 2020, Santa Fe, NM
ISBN 978-0-9967835-9-0

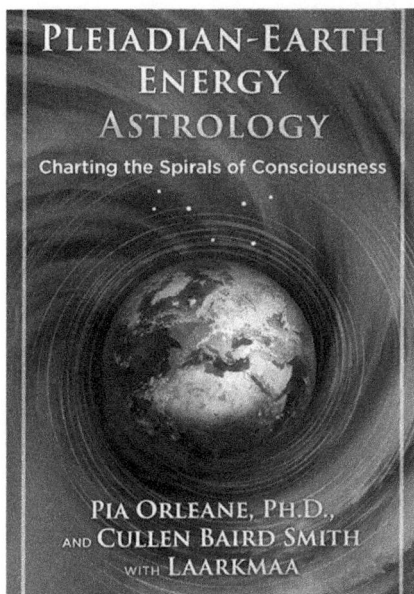

PLEIADIAN-EARTH ENERGY ASTROLOGY
Charting the Spirals of Consciousness

by Pia Orleane, Ph.D. & Cullen Baird Smith
Inner Traditions/Bear & Company, 2018
Rochester, VT
ISBN 978-1-59143-309-5

Yearly Gold Award-winning

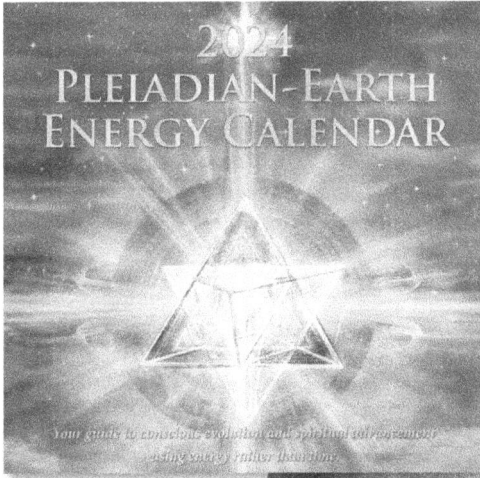

PLEIADIAN-EARTH ENERGY CALENDAR
by Pia Orleane, Ph.D. & Cullen Baird Smith
2019, 2020, 2021, 2022, 2023, 2024; Onewater Press, Santa Fe, NM
https://www.laarkmaa.com/pleiadian-earth-energy-calendar

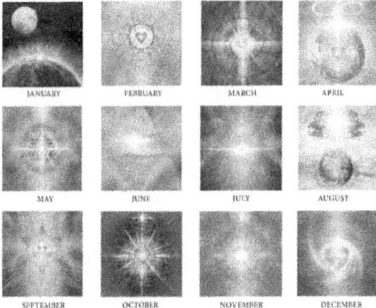

Coalition for Visionary Resources
Gold Award-winning card deck,

THE ORIGINAL PLEIADIAN WISDOM
ORACLE CARDS
by Pia Orleane, Ph.D. & Cullen Baird Smith
Onewater Press, 2022
Santa Fe, NM
ISBN 978-1-7367035-9-5